Chofetz Chaim

Desirer of Life

Rabbi

Israel Meir Kagan
Ha'Kohen

The Rabbi of
Radin

SimchatChaim.com

There is no known book without mistakes. Therefore, I ask in every language of application if anyone has any questions, comments, clarifications, corrections, please send to: book@simchatchaim.com

All material used in this section may not be used for commercial purposes, but only for study and teaching.
To get this book or books and information Email me at:

book@simchatchaim.com

Copyright ©All Rights Reserved to
www.simchatchaim.com

YB"S©All rights reserved to the Editor

Second Edition 2023

CHOFETZ   Contents   CHAIM

TABLE OF CONTENTS

Page	Contents
3.	**Preface**
15.	Introduction to the Laws of the Prohibition of **Lashon Hara** [slander] and **Rechiluth** [Gossip]
15.	Opening Comments
21.	Negative Commandments
30.	Positive Commandments
42.	Curses
45.	**Part One**
	The Prohibition Against **Lashon Hara** [slander]
45.	Principle 1
50.	Principle 2
60.	Principle 3
65.	Principle 4
79.	Principle 5
90.	Principle 6
99.	Principle 7
108.	Principle 8
119.	Principle 9
123.	Principle 10

139.	**Part Two**

The Prohibition Against **Rechiluth** [Gossip]

139.	Principle 1
145.	Principle 2
148.	Principle 3
150.	Principle 4
152.	Principle 5
158.	Principle 6
166.	Principle 7
170.	Principle 8
172.	Principle 9

189.	**Illustrations**

189.	Illustration 1
190.	Illustration 2
191.	Illustration 3
192.	Illustration 4
193.	Illustration 5
196.	Illustration 6
198.	Illustration 7
199.	Illustration 8
201.	Illustration 9
202.	Illustration 10
203.	Illustration 11

Preface

Blessed is the Lord, the God of Israel, who has separated us from all the peoples and given us His Torah, and brought us to the holy land so that we merit fulfilling all of His Mitzvoth. His sole intent was for our good alone so that through this we become holy unto Him as is written - So[1] that you remember and do all of My Mitzvoth and be holy unto your God. And so that it be in our power to receive the effluence of His good and the abundance of His lovingkindness in this world and in the world to come, as it is written - And[2] now - O Israel, what does your God demand of you - Only this - to revere your God to walk only in divine paths, to love and to serve your God - with all your heart and soul. keeping[3] God's commandments and laws which I enjoin upon you today, for your good. See the **R'amban** there to the effect that - **to do good unto you** reverts to- **What does the Lord your God ask of you.**

And not only has He given us His special treasure, but He has also commanded us not to forsake it, as it is written - For[4] a goodly acquisition have I given you, do not forsake My Torah. Unlike the way of flesh and blood, who, if he gives his friend a fine gift, and the other does not deport himself with it correctly, and it is not beloved in his eyes, he pines for the day that his friend will abandon it altogether so that he can take it back for himself. Not so is the way of our God. For He established

---

[1] Numbers 15:40
[2] Devarim 10:12
[3] Devarim 10:12
[4] Mishlei 4:2

for us prophets in all the generations of the first Temple to return us to the good. And even in the days of the second Temple, when - in our many sins. Israel descended from its pristine holiness, and when they lacked five things which obtained in the first Temple ark, ark-cover, and cherubim, the Heavenly fire, the Shechinah, prophecy, and the **Urim**[5] **Vetumim** - notwithstanding this, when we were on our land and had a Temple, we could fulfill all the Mitzvoth of the Torah, and thereby bring to perfection all of the spiritual components within us - the soul like the body, possessing 248 **organs** and 365 **sinews** as stated by Rabbi[6] Chaim Vital.

But at the end of the days of the Second Temple, **Sinath Chinam** [Hate for no reason] and **Lashon Hara** [slander] increased among us - in our many sins, for which reason the Temple was destroyed and we were exiled from our land. Though the Talmud[7] calls it **Sinath Chinam** [Hate for no reason], **Lashon Hara** [slander] is included, proceeding, as it does, from **Sinah** [Hate]. If this were not the case, they would not have been punished so severely, as the Talmud there concludes - This is to teach you that **Sinath Chinam** [Hate for no reason] is equivalent to idolatry, illicit relations, and the spilling of blood. And we find the same in The Talmud[8] with respect to **Lashon Hara** [slander], and, likewise, in the discussion in the Talmud[9] itself. And from then until now, every day, we hope and pray before the Holy One Blessed

---

[5] Yoma 21b
[6] Sha'arei Kedushah of, Chapter One
[7] Yoma 9b and Yerushalmi 1:5
[8] Arachin 15b
[9] Yoma 9b and 23a

be He that He draws us near - to Him, as He assured us in His holy Torah and through His prophets many times. But our prayer is not accepted by Him, as **Chazal** [Sages] have said in the Talmud - From[10] the day of the destruction of the Temple, a wall of iron separates Israel from their Father in heaven.

And, in truth, not against Him God forbid is our plant, but against ourselves, for it, the redemption is not beyond His powers, as is written - No[11] God's arm is not too short to save Or God's ear too dull to hear. But[12] your iniquities have been a barrier Between you and your God Your sins have made the divine face turn away As God refuses to hear you. And we find in the Talmud[13] - That in the days of Rabbi Yehoshua ben Levi, he was told that the Messiah would come? The answer to him was this verse - Today[14] if you hearkened to His voice. Even though the time of the exile decreed for Israel one thousand years, corresponding to the one thousand years **day** of the Holy One Blessed be He, had not yet passed. In spite of this, the power of repentance would have annulled the decree. How much more so, more than eight hundred years after the end of that - One-thousand-year, **day** should the Messiah come if we repented? The fault is ours alone - that with our many sins, we do not allow Him to repose His Shechinah in our midst.

And if we carefully searched our ways - which of the sins have primarily caused the length of our exile? - we would find them to be many, but the sin of **Lashon**

---

[10] Berachoth 32b
[11] Isaiah 59:1
[12] Isaiah 59:2
[13] Sanhedrin 98a
[14] Tehillim 95:6

Hara [slander] above all, for several reasons. First, for it was the major cause of our exile - as related in the aforementioned Talmud. This being so, as long as we do not undertake to correct this sin, how can there be a redemption, the sin being so severe as to have caused us to be exiled from our land? How much more so will it not allow us to return to our land?

Furthermore, is it not well known that exile had already been decreed upon us because of the act of the spies - *They[15] grumbled in their tents and disobeyed the Lord. So[16] He raised His hand in oath to make them fall in the wilderness. To[17] disperse their offspring among the nations and scatter them through the lands.* as **R'ashi** and the **R'amban** explain[18] there. And the sin of the spies - was it not that of **Lashon Hara** [slander]. As it says in Talmud[19]. Therefore, it is imperative that we correct this sin before redemption can take place.

And[20] we find it explicitly stated that it was this sin which caused the Jews to be worked by the Egyptians with back-breaking labor. And in the Midrash - *The[21] Holy One Blessed be He said - In this world, because there was **Lashon Hara** [slander] among you, I removed My Shechinah from you, but in the next world.* And in the Torah - *And[22] He became a King in Yeshurun when the heads of the people were gathered together as one, the tribes of Israel.* Which **R'ashi** interprets, as per **Sifrei** -

---

[15] Tehillim 106:25
[16] Tehillim 106:26
[17] Tehillim 106:27
[18] Bamidbar 14
[19] Arachin 15a
[20] Shemoth 2:14 and see R'ashi there
[21] Devarim Rabbah 6:14
[22] Devarim 33:5

When is He a King in Israel? Specifically, when the tribes of Israel are united and not divided into factions - which factions are well known to be the result of **Lashon Hara** [slander].

And, aside from this, how can the hoped-for blessings of the Holy One Blessed be He repose upon us when, in our many sins, we have become habituated to this sin? Is there not an explicit curse on this in the Torah - Cursed[23] is he who strikes his neighbor in secret, which refers to **Lashon Hara** [slander], as **R'ashi** explains there - aside from the other curses which are superadded to this, as will be shown at the end of this preface?

In addition, is it not seen from the aforementioned Talmud[24] that this sin is of infinite severity, so much so that they have branded its practitioners as heretics? And in the Talmud[25] - it is stated that punishment is exacted for this sin in this world, with the **principal** remaining for punishment in the world to come.

See the end of this preface and my book **Shmirath Halashon**, where we have transcribed all the relevant citations from the Talmud, the Midrash, and the holy Zohar. If one scrutinizes them carefully, the hairs of his head will stand on end.

And it seems clear that the Torah was severe with this sin because he the speaker of **Lashon Hara** [slander] arouses the Great Adversary against Israel and thereby kills many people in many lands. Consider the language of the holy Zohar[26] - There is a certain spirit appointed over all these speakers of **Lashon Hara** [slander], which,

---

[23] Devarim 27:24
[24] Arachin 15a
[25] Yerushalmi Peah 1:1
[26] Zohar Shemoth Pekudei 264b

when men are aroused to **Lashon Hara** [slander], there is likewise aroused that malevolent, unclean spirit above, which is called **Sachsusa** [contention]. Presiding over that arousal of **Lashon Hara** [slander] initiated by men, he rises on high and causes - by that arousal of **Lashon Hara** [slander] death, sword, and slaughter in the world. Woe unto those who arouse this malevolent force by not guarding their mouth and their tongue, giving no thought to it, not knowing that on this lower arousal depends the higher arousal, both for good and for evil. And all of them arouse this Great Serpent to be an adversary against the world. And all this, because of the **Lashon Hara** [slander] arousal initiated below.

And we can say that this is the intent of the aforementioned Talmud - All[27] who speak **Lashon Hara** [slander] magnify transgression until the heavens, as it is written - They[28] set their mouth in the heavens and their tongue walks the earth. That is, even though his tongue walks the earth, he sets his mouth against Heaven. And thus, do we find it in Midrash - That[29] the **Lashon Hara** [slander] that he speaks rises against the Throne of Glory. We can hereby derive some idea of the greatness of the destruction wrought against Israel by the - **men of the tongue**.

Another reason for the severity of this transgression is - When a man taints his tongue with forbidden things, he prevents all expressions of sanctity which leave his mouth thereafter from rising on high. As stated by the holy Zohar[30] - And upon this malevolent

---

[27] Arachin 15a
[28] Tehillim 73:9
[29] Tanna D'bei Eliyahu Zuta 18
[30] Zohar Shemoth Pekudei 264b

spirit there are contingent other inciters of **Din** [the law], which are designated to seize upon expressions of evil or of foulness which issue from a man's mouth, which are followed by expressions of holiness. Woe unto them. Woe to their lives. These men cause those other arousers of **Din** [the law] to prevail and to taint the Holy Place. Woe to them in this world and woe to them in the world to come. For these other spirits of uncleanliness take this evil expression that has issued from his mouth, and sully the expression of holiness which follows, so that it is not ascribed to him, and the power of holiness has been, as it were, attenuated. Is it not evident from the holy Zohar that in such an instance all our words of Torah and prayer stand suspended in the air and do not arise on high? Whence, then, will they come to our aid for the coming of the Messiah and the like?

And when we delve more deeply into this matter, we find that in addition to its being a grave transgression in itself, it undermines all the upper worlds and darkens and lessens their light. For it is the habit of many men to redouble violation of this negative commandment many hundreds and thousands of times in the course of their lives. For even a small sin, when it is repeated many times, becomes like thick cart-ropes, as Isaiah exhorted - Woe[31] unto those who draw forth iniquity with cords of deceit and who draw forth sin as thick as cart-ropes. This is analogous to the instance of a silken strand which is redoubled hundreds of times. How much more so is this sin of **Lashon Hara** [slander], which is extremely grave in itself and which countless men tend to repeat many thousands of times in the course of their lives without

---

[31] Isaiah 5:18

taking it upon themselves to guard themselves against it - how much more so is the corresponding, undermining of the worlds, above without limit.

And I sought to understand this - Why is it that this negative commandment has become insignificant in the eyes of so many men? And I reflected that this must be so for several reasons, affecting the common people on one hand and the Torah scholars on the other. The common people do not even know that the prohibition of **Lashon Hara** [slander] applies to what is true as well as to what is untrue, and the Torah scholars, even though they know for a certainty that it applies to what is true as well - some of them are misled by the **Yetzer Hara** [evil inclination] in a variety of ways. One of these - The **Yetzer Hara** [evil inclination] puts it immediately into his head that the one he is speaking of is a flatterer, and says to him - It is a mitzvah to expose the flatterers and the evil-doers. At other times it says to him - Is not that man - you are speaking of, a stirrer-up of strife, about whom it is permitted to speak **Lashon Hara** [slander]? And sometimes it tempts him with the **Halachoth** [the Law] permit of **Apei Telata** [next to three people] **Lashon Hara** [slander] spoken in the presence of three, and, sometimes, of **Apei Mara** [in front of those who are talking about him] - convincing him that he would speak thus even to the victim's face. And the **Yetzer Hara** [evil inclination] provides him with the relevant citations, see below[32]. And sometimes he appeals to the nature of what is being said - That is that it is not in the category of **Lashon Hara** [slander] what many, in our many sins, are

---

[32] Principles 2, 3, and 8

prone to do, publicizing one as not being wise as will be explained below[33].

In sum, the **Yetzer Hara** [evil inclination] in respect to **Lashon Hara** [slander] acts in one of two ways: It convinces the speaker that what he says is not **Lashon Hara** [slander], or that the Torah did not forbid speaking **Lashon Hara** [slander] against such and such a man.

And if the **Yetzer Hara** [evil inclination] sees that in these ways he cannot prevail over the man, he deceives him in reverse, being so stringent with him in the area of **Lashon Hara** [slander] until he sees everything as entering into the category of **Lashon Hara** [slander], to the extent that he sees it as impossible to live life thus constrained unless he separates entirely from the affairs of the world - as per the device of the primal subtle serpent, who said to **Eve** - Did[34] God really say do not eat from all the trees of the garden? when, in reality, he had interdicted only the Tree of Knowledge.

Add to this that many men lack a fundamental understanding of the prohibition of receiving **Lashon Hara** [slander] - that it applies even to believe it in the heart and not only to repeat it though one is permitted to **suspect** it to be true - As it says in Talmud[35]. The same is true of many similar instances in the area of receiving **Lashon Hara** [slander] and of **Rechiluth** [Gossip], which cannot be specified here. And they also do not know how to make amends if they have transgressed the

---

[33] Principle 3
[34] Genesis 3:1
[35] Niddah 61a

prohibition of speaking **Lashon Hara** [slander] and of receiving it.

Because of these reasons, things have come to such a pass that one says whatever enters his mouth to say, without first considering that it might enter the category of **Rechiluth** [Gossip] and **Lashon Hara** [slander]. In our many sins, we have become so habituated to this sin that in the eyes of many men it is not considered a sin at all - even if he would say something which is apparent to everyone as absolute **Lashon Hara** [slander] and **Rechiluth** [Gossip], as when he would speak of his friend and demean him to the very ends of degradation. And if one asked him - Why did you speak **Lashon Hara** [slander] and **Rechiluth** [Gossip]? he would think in his heart that he - his chastiser thought to make him a **fanatic** Tzaddik or **Chasid** [righteous person], and he would not accept his words at all, regarding this **Lashon Hara** [slander] and **Rechiluth** [Gossip], in our many sins, as completely insignificant.

And all these proceeds, for the most part - from the laws of **Lashon Hara** [slander] and **Rechiluth** [Gossip] not having been gathered into one spot, where there could be elucidated their nature and application, in principle and in practice. Instead, they are scattered in the Talmud and in the **Rishonim** [the first Sages ones]. And even the Rambam in the seventh chapter of **Hilchoth Deoth** and **Rabbeinu Yonah** in the **S'haarei Teshuvah**, who have paved the way for us in this area, have, nonetheless, been very terse, as is the way of the **Rishonim** [the first Sages ones]. And there are also many **Dinim** [the laws] that are not mentioned in their words, as will be seen within.

And let the reader, my brother, know that for even

the simplest thing found therein, I have indicated its source in the book **Be'er Mayim Chayim**, so that it be clear before the eyes of all that I have not written this book according to the parameters of **Chasiduth** [saintliness], but according to the parameters of **Din** [the law].

For the **Din** [the law] flows from them - these sources. And all who judge me by the scales of merit, may the Source of life judge them by the scales of merit. I have also written for this book a long, extensive foreword, explicating several negative and positive commandments frequently transgressed by those who do not guard themselves against this bitter sin of **Lashon Hara** [slander] and **Rechiluth** [Gossip]. May the Lord grant that the **Yetzer** [inclination] be smitten when he the transgressor realizes the extent of the havoc and the harm wrought by his speech.

Aside from this, the following Midrash is well known - If[36] you have labored much in their - the sage's words, the Holy One Blessed be He removes the **Yetzer Hara** [evil inclination] from you whereupon I said to myself - Possibly, if they study this book, which is gathered from all the words of the **Rishonim** [the first Sages ones] on this subject, and reflect upon them, the **Yetzer Hara** [evil inclination] for this sin will not prevail so much over them. And, as a matter of course, if one starts to remove himself from this sin, he will come to remove himself from it entirely. For in this sin, habit plays a great part, and in the Talmud - One[37] who comes to purify himself is assisted by the Lord. And in this

---

[36] Midrash Rabbah 14:4
[37] Yoma 38b

merit, may the Redeemer - The Messiah. come[38] to Zion, speedily, in our days, **Amen**.

---

[38] Isaiah 50:29

CHOFETZ   Introduction   CHAIM

Introduction to the Laws of the Prohibition of

Lashon Hara [slander] and Rechiluth [Gossip]

Opening Comments

In the Blessed One's love for His people Israel and His great desire for their good - to the point of calling them **sons, the portion of the Lord**, and **inheritance**, along with many other terms of affection which show His great love for Israel, as is written - I[1] have loved You, said the Lord, etc., He distanced them from all forms of evil, especially from **Lashon Hara** [slander] and received. For it is these which bring men to quarrels and contention and which very often can lead to the spilling of blood, as the Rambam wrote - Even[2] though there are no **malkoth** [stripes] for the transgression of this negative commandment, it is a great sin, which leads to the killing of many souls in Israel, for which reason it. Do[3] not go tale-bearing among your people. Is followed by - Do not stand idly by the blood of your brother. As evidenced by the episode of - Doeg[4] Ha'Adomi and Nov, the city of priests.

    Some additional great evils brought about by this despicable trait - It is well known that the sin of the primal serpent was brought about by the lashon hara that it spoke against the Holy One Blessed be He, saying to Eve - He [God] ate from this tree, the Tree of Knowledge and

---

[1] Malachi 1:2
[2] Hilchoth Deoth 4:1
[3] Vayikra 19:16
[4] Samuel-A 22:9

created the world, by which Eve was enticed to do likewise in the Talmud - The[5] serpent was **intimate** with Eve and injected **Zuhamah** [pollution] into her - hence, the sin of illicit relations, and also death to all mankind - hence, the spilling of blood. And through this **Lashon Hara** [slander], it induced Adam and Eve to transgress the will of the Holy One Blessed be He. It follows that one who speaks lashon hara adopts its the serpent's trait, which undermines the creation.

And the descent of Israel into Egypt, too, stemmed initially from this from **Lashon Hara** [slander], as is written - And[6] Joseph brought evil report of them, the sons of Leah to their father, whence it was decreed by Heaven, measure for measure, that he be sold into slavery, his having accused them of calling their brothers from the maidservant's **slaves** as is written[7] Though Joseph had a **Heter** [halachic license] for bringing this **evil report**, as the exegetes explain, it is to be noted that this **Heter** did not avail him, and he was sold into slavery. And again, the entire reason for our present exile is the sin of the spies - And[8] they murmured in their tents against the land. They hearkened not to the word of the Lord. And He lifted up His hand in oath against them… to scatter them in the lands, as R'ashi explains there, and as the **Ramban** wrote[9]. And it is stated in Talmud[10] that the sin of the spies was essentially **Lashon Hara** [slander], their giving out an evil report of the land. And

---

[5] Sabbath 146a
[6] Bereshith 37:2
[7] Bereshith Rabbah 84:7 and Yerushalmi Peah 1:1
[8] Tehillim 6:25-27
[9] Bamidbar 14:1
[10] Arachin 15a

because they then, on the eve of the ninth of Av cried a **vain** cry, it the ninth of Av was decreed for them as a **crying** for the generations, the destruction of both Temples, etc. And countless other evils befell us because of this grave sin. For all the sages of Israel who were killed by King Yannai in the days of Shimon ben Shetach, the brother-in-law of King Yannai, were also killed because of the sin of **Rechiluth** [Gossip] stated in Talmud - And[11] the murder of the Tanna Rabbi Elazar Hamodai, which also contributed to the destruction of Betar, was likewise caused by **Rechiluth** [Gossip] which was spoken against him before Ben Koziva[12].

And because of the gravity of the evils found in this evil trait, the Torah exhorted us specifically against it by the negative commandment - Do[13] not go talebearing among your people. As shall be explained below as opposed to anger, cruelty, and levity and the other corrupt traits, which even though they undermine the majesty of the soul and its form, and they were alluded to in many places in the Torah, as explained in the words of Sages - with all this, there is no explicit negative commandment against them as there is against **Rechiluth** [Gossip] in the count of **Taryag** [the 613 commandments] of the Torah. And we shall note yet another reason for the Torah's exhorting us explicitly against these - **Lashon Hara** [slander] and **Rechiluth** [Gossip]. For when we analyze them in truth, we find them to include almost all the negative and positive commandments which obtain between a man and his neighbor and many between a man

---

[11] Kiddushin 66a
[12] Eichah Rabbah 2:4
[13] Vayikra 19:16

and his Maker, as we shall explain, God willing. It is for this reason that the Torah exhorted us against these explicitly, so that we not become enmeshed in this evil snare. I shall explain this with the help of the Blessed One. And from this there shall follow, incidentally, great benefit Against many other **Halachoth** [the Law]. And also, perhaps, because of this, the **Yetzer** [inclination] will be smitten when he the transgressor, perceives the great havoc and harm wrought by his speech. And here I begin, with the help of Him who grants a man knowledge. First, we must know the principles of these **Halakhoth** [the Law] of **Lashon Hara** [slander] and **Rechiluth** [Gossip]. **Lashon Hara** [slander] is speaking disparagingly against one's friend, and **Rechiluth** [Gossip], tells one the evil thing that his friend has spoken against him or done against him. The principles - It **Lashon Hara** [slander] and **Rechiluth** [Gossip] are forbidden even if true, as will be explained below, please God, in the name of all the **Poskim** [Halachic Rulings]. Also, the prohibition of **Lashon Hara** [slander] and **Rechiluth** [Gossip] applies both in the object's presence and not in his presence. Also, there is no difference between speaking and receiving **Lashon Hara** [slander] and **Rechiluth** [Gossip], all of which we shall explain further. A **receiver** of **Lashon Hara** [slander] is one who believes in his heart what is told him by his friend even if he does not abet him in the telling but only believes in his heart the **Lashon Hara** [slander] and **Rechiluth** [Gossip] that he has heard. If he does believe it, he is called - **The bearer of a false report** and transgresses - Do[14] not bear a false report. All of these principles have roots and

---

[14] Shemoth 23:1

branches, as in the other parts of the Torah. May the Lord grant that we know them comprehensively.

And know that whenever we write that he transgresses both the negative and the positive commandments and the three **curses** attaching to them, which we shall mention and elucidate below, our intent is both **Lashon Hara** [slander] and **Rechiluth** [Gossip], and both what is false and what is true. And this is what we shall refer to in the book - **Be'er Mayim Chayim** as **in the first four modes** unless we explicitly state that it applies only in one of them. And it shall then remain necessary for us only to explain with respect to all of the negative or positive commandments whether they apply in the object's presence or not in his presence, or to the speaker or to the receiver.

And those negative or positive commandments which include all of the modes, I shall refer to, in short, in the **Be'er Mayim Chaim** as - In all the eight modes. that is - **Lashon Hara** [slander] and **Rechiluth** [Gossip], in his presence or not in his presence, both to the speaker and to the receiver, and both if false or if true. Remember these things, for I will not reiterate them in the introduction.

First, we shall explain how many negative commandments one transgresses in the speaking of **Lashon Hara** [slander] and **Rechiluth** [Gossip], and then, how many positive commandments. Then, how many **curses** he brings upon himself, and, further, how many great **Issurim** [prohibitions] result from this.

I shall divide this introduction into two parts; the first, to be called **Makor Chaim**, and a super commentary around it called **Be'er Mayim Chayim**. The reason for these names I have given in the preface. In the **Be'er Mayim Chayim** it will be made clear to which mode each negative or positive commandment applies, along with some other **Halachoth** [the Law]. This I begin with the help of Him who grants a man knowledge.

Negative Commandments

1. One who bears tales against his friend transgresses a negative commandment - Do[15] not go talebearing among your people. What is talebearing? **Loading oneself** with words and going from one to another, saying - This is what **Ploni** [so and so] said about you - This and this is what I heard **Ploni** [so and so] did to you. Although what he says may be true, it destroys the world. And there is a sin much greater than this - **Lashon Hara** [slander], which is included in this negative commandment. And that is speaking disparagingly of one's friend, even if what is said is true. But one who speaks falsely - about his friend, is referred to as a **Motzi Shem Ra** [one who spreads an evil report].

2. And the speaker or the receiver of **Lashon Hara** [slander] also transgresses - Do[16] not **Tissa** [receive] a false report, which can also be read as - Do not **Tassi** [spread] a false report, so that this negative commandment includes both, the speaker and the receiver.

3. And the speaker also transgresses - Be[17] heedful of the plague-spot of leprosy to take great care, which Sifra[18] interprets as - Take great care, not to forget to be heedful of **Lashon Hara** [slander] so that leprosy not come upon you as it came upon Miriam for speaking **Lashon Hara**

---

[15] Vayikra 19:16
[16] Shemoth 23:1
[17] Devarim 24:8
[18] Sifra 1:3

[slander] against Moshe.

4. And both the speaker and the receiver transgress - And[19] before the blind man does not place a stumbling block. Each one - both the speaker and the listener, places a stumbling block before his friend to transgress explicit negative commandments in the Torah. But there is a difference between the speaker and the listener in this regard. For the speaker transgresses this negative commandment both whether the listeners are many or few. Even more so, the more the listeners, the more the speaker transgresses this negative commandment, placing a stumbling block before many people. Not so the receiver. It is possible that he does not transgress this negative commandment unless he himself hears the **Lashon Hara** [slander] or the **Rechiluth** [Gossip] from him - the speaker, at the moment so that if he had left him, he would have no one to relate his **Lashon Hara** [slander] to. But if there are, besides him, different listeners at the time, it is possible that the hearer does not transgress this negative commandment, but only others mentioned in this introduction – see the book **Be'er Mayim Chayim**. And all this, if he came after the **recital** had started. But the first listener - even though others arrived afterward - certainly transgresses in all eight modes, for the **Issur** [prohibition] was initiated through him. In any event, one must take great heed of such companions, not to sit with them, for **above** they are all inscribed as **a company of wickedness**. And thus, is it found in the will of Rabbi Eliezer Hagadol to Hyrcanus, his son - My[20] son, do not

---

[19] Vayikra 19:14
[20] Midrashim of Rabbi Eliezer 55

sit with the companies of those who speak ill of their friends, for when their words rise on high, they are inscribed in a book and all who stand there are described as - **a wicked company**.

5. And the speaker of **Lashon Hara** [slander] also transgresses - Take[21] heed unto yourself lest you forget the Lord your God. Which is an exhortation to the proud of spirit, for since he mocks and ridicules his friend, he apparently considers himself wise and **a man among men**. For if he knew his own faults, he would not deride his friend. And the statement of Sages in the Talmud on the severity of the sin of pride is well known - Because[22] of it his dust does not wake for the resurrection, he is considered an idolator, the Shechinah wails over him, and he is called **an abomination**. And, especially, if in shaming his friend he honors himself, he certainly transgresses this negative commandment, aside from our Rabbis in their holy spirit having **cut him off** from the world to come, saying in the Talmud - One[23] who honors himself by the shame of his friend has no share in the world to come.

6. The speaker and the receiver of **Lashon Hara** [slander] also transgress - And[24] you shall not profane My holy name. In that there is no lust or physical pleasure to cause his **Yetzer** [inclination] to intensify itself over him so that this sin is regarded as rebellion and blatant divesting oneself of the yoke of Heaven, and he profanes the name

---

[21] Devarim 8:11
[22] Sotah 4b
[23] Yerushalmi Chagigah 12:1
[24] Vayikra 22:32

of Heaven thereby. This, even in the instance of a plain Jew, how much more so in the instance of a man of eminence, whom they all look up to for guidance speaking **Lashon Hara** [slander], where the name of Heaven is certainly profaned. And how much more so, if this sin were committed in public, would it be extremely grave, the transgressor being called - **A desecrator of the name of God in public**.

7. And sometimes the speaker transgresses - You[25] shall not hate your brother in your heart. As when he **speaks peace** with his friend in his presence, and denigrates him before others when he is not in his presence. And much more, does he transgress, if he explicitly charges them not to go and inform him, in which instance he, of a certainty, transgresses this negative commandment.

8-9. Sometimes the speaker also transgresses - You[26] shall not take revenge and you shall not bear a grudge. As when the speaker bears hatred towards him, having asked him to lend him something and having been denied, and, thereafter, seeing something demeaning in him, he publicizes it before others. From the beginning, he transgresses - **You shall not bear a grudge**, by bearing the grudge in his heart. And later, when he takes revenge and reveals the demeaning thing, he has seen in him, he transgresses - **You shall not take revenge**. But he must wipe the thing from his heart.

10. And if one arises and testifies against another by

---

[25] Leviticus 19:17
[26] Vayikra 19:18

himself before **Beth-Bin** [Court] concerning something forbidden, since no benefit can result from this vis-à-vis monetary obligation, imposition of an oath, or invalidation of the other's status of **Kashruth** [Kosher] since he is only a single witness in the matter, the only thing he **accomplishes** by this is giving the other a bad name, and he also transgresses the negative commandment of - One[27] witness shall not testify against a man for every transgression and for every sin. and **Beth-Din** [Court] must punish him with stripes for this.

11. And all this that we have written applies to one who speaks singly or who listens singly, but if he joins himself to a company of wicked men and speakers of **Lashon Hara** [slander] to tell them or to listen to them, he also transgresses - Do[28] not incline after many for evil. which is an exhortation not to agree with or even join with evildoers, though they are many. where I have cited Pirkei D'Rabbi Eliezer[29] on his will to his son in this regard.

12. And if he nurtures a quarrel in his speaking, he transgresses - And[30] he shall not be as **Korach** and as his congregation, which is an exhortation against nurturing a quarrel in the Talmud[31].

13. And many times, another negative commandment is transgressed. For very often one's friend is demeaned for

---

[27] Devarim 19:15
[28] Shemoth 23:2
[29] Midrashim of Rabbi Eliezer 55
[30] Bamidbar 17:5
[31] Sanhedrin 110a

his early deeds, for a family trait, for the paucity of his learning, or for his mediocre work, each man according to his situation, things being said to him which anger and confound him and against which he has no defense. Even if this transpired between the two of them alone no one else being present, he the speaker transgresses - And[32] you shall not wrong. One man his fellow. Which refers to verbal wronging in the Talmud - How[33] much more so if this occurred in the company of others. It emerges, then, that if one slights his friend both through **Rechiluth** [Gossip] or through **Lashon Hara** [slander], before him alone or before others, aside from transgressing the negative commandment of **Lashon Hara** [slander] and **Rechiluth** [Gossip], as stated above, he also transgresses this negative commandment.

14. And if he demeans another thus, with such words and the like, before him alone and before others, to the extent that his face changes color with shame, he transgresses also - Reprove[34] Reprove your fellow and do not bear sin because of him. The Torah exhorted one hereby not to shame his fellow Jew, even for the sake of reproof and even between him and the other alone. That is, not to speak so sharply to him that he shames him - How much more so should he not do so, if not for the sake of reproof and if he is in the presence of others? And all this, if it did not take place in public, but if he **whitens** his face with shame in public, Sages have already **cut him off** from the world to come, in the Talmud are saying says - One[35] who

---

[32] Vayikra 25:17
[33] Bava Metzia 58b
[34] Vayikra 19:17
[35] Bava Metzia 59a

whitens his friend's face in public has no share in the world to come.

15. And if the other were an orphan or a widow, even if they were wealthy, and he spoke demandingly before them, he also transgresses - Every[36] widow and orphan you shall not afflict. the Torah exhorting hereby not to taunt them or sadden their heart with any kind of sorrow. The punishment for this is explicit in the Torah - And[37] My wrath shall burn, and I shall kill you by the sword, and your wives will be widows, and your children, orphans.

16. And sometimes he transgresses also the **Issur** [prohibition] of flattery, which is to many **Geonim** [Genius] as H'aReem, Baal Hatosfoth, and Hagaon Rabbi Shlomoh ben G'virol an absolute negative commandment - And[38] you shall not flatter the men of the land. That is if his intent in speaking **Lashon Hara** [slander] and **Rechiluth** [Gossip] is to flatter the listener, whom he knows to bear hatred to the one spoken about, and thereby, to find favor in his eyes - an egregious sin - is it not enough that he does not fulfill the Mitzvah of **Reproof** - a positive commandment in the Torah, to reprove him for the hatred he bears his friend, that he also strengthens the hatred that already exists among them. And through him - the speaker, he - the listener will persist in his wrong more and more so that more quarrels and wrongs will Result God forbid. And know that this

---

[36] Shemoth 22:21
[37] Shemoth 22:23
[38] Bamidbar 35:33

the following sin - in our many sins, is widespread. That is, when one speaks demandingly of his friend often, the listener, knowing that what is being said is unfounded, nevertheless nods his head in agreement and he, too, **smoothes over** the thing with his tongue, adding some words of taint. For the speaker is sometimes a man of means, or the like, from whom he receives favors, or who he fears will regard him as unwise, or the like for remaining silent. And, therefore, the **Yetzer** [inclination] will entice him, too, to concur in this. But know, my brother, that this, too, is essentially a transgression of the negative commandment of flattery - even if he adds but a few words - as is explained in the book **Be'er Mayim Chayim**. And in this regard, it is written - And[39] put a knife to your throat against speaking **Lashon Hara** [slander] if you are a man of spirit. And one must rather expose himself to danger than bring his soul to such a sin. According to the Torah, every man under such circumstances must, in any event, strengthen himself not to abet him - the speaker even by so much as one movement which would cause it to appear that he concurs with what he is saying. And in this connection, we can understand the words of Sages in the Mishna - It[40] is better to be called a fool all of one's days than to be wicked one moment before the Almighty. And this, even if he knows that his words of reproof will not be accepted by the speaker, for otherwise, he certainly must reprove him for this, too as will be explained, God willing, in **Halachoth** [the Law] **Lashon Hara** [slander].

---

[39] Mishlei 23:2
[40] Eiduyoth 5:6

17. And sometimes there is yet another negative commandment which is found to be transgressed in our many sins - speaking **Lashon Hara** [slander] against someone in anger, and at the same time, cursing him - sometimes even by the Name even if in the vernacular. In doing so, one transgresses an absolute negative commandment - Do[41] not curse a deaf man. The meaning being **even** a deaf man - how much more so, one who is not deaf, as explained in **Shulchan**[42] **Aruch**. We have hereby enumerated seventeen negative commandments which are often attendant upon **Lashon Hara** [slander] and **Rechiluth** [Gossip] - even if he speaks only to a Jew. For if he slanders a Jew to a non-Jew, the **Issur** [prohibition] is greater and graver, sometimes entering into the category of **Massur** [informing], as we shall explain, God willing, in **Halachoth** [the Law] **Lashon Hara** [slander]. And transgression of many of the aforementioned negative commandments are subject to death at the hands of Heaven - such as demeaning a widow or an orphan or profaning the Name. And many of them have implications for the world to come, such as **whitening** the face of one's friend in public or honoring oneself in the shame of his friend. This, in the instance of one who habituates himself to this grave transgression of **Lashon Hara** [slander] and **Rechiluth** [Gossip], all of which will be explained below, God willing.

---

[41] Vayikra 19:14
[42] Choshen Mishpat 27:1

Positive Commandments

And now I shall begin, with the help of the Blessed Lord to explain how many positive commandments one transgresses in speaking **Lashon Hara** [slander] and **Rechiluth** [Gossip], as we projected above. One who bears tales against his friend, aside from transgressing the negative commandments we mentioned above, also transgresses several positive commandments, which I shall explain, with the help of the Blessed One, one by one.

1. He transgresses thereby - Remember[43] what the Lord your God did to Miriam on the way when you went out of Egypt. The Torah exhorted us hereby that we mention verbally, always, the great punishment - leprosy, that the Blessed Lord brought upon the **Tzadeketh**, Miriam the prophetess - who spoke only about her brother, whom she loved as her soul, whom she raised on her knees, and for whom she endangered her life, to rescue him from the Nile. And she did not speak in the denigration of him but only compared him to other prophets. And she did not speak so to his face to shame him, and not in public, but only to her brother Aaron, privately. And the Moshe was not offended by all this, as is written - And[44] the man Moshe was extremely humble, more than any man on the face of the earth - In spite of which all her good deeds did not avail her and she was punished with leprosy for this. How much more so will other people, the fools, who are

---

[43] Devarim 24:9
[44] Bamidbar 12:3

prolix in speaking - Great and awesome things. against their friends, and be severely punished for this.

2. And he the speaker of Lashon Hara [slander] also transgresses - And[45] you shall love your neighbor as yourself. Whereby we have been commanded to be as solicitous for our friend's money as we are for our own, and to be solicitous of his honor, and to speak in his praise, as we are solicitous for our own honor. And if one speaks or receives **Lashon Hara** [slander] and **Rechiluth** [Gossip] against his friend, though it be true, it is apparent that he does not love him at all - how much more so is he in violation of - as yourself. And the great proof of this, that he is in violation of **as yourself** is as follows - Does not every man know his own shortcomings? - in spite of which he would not want his friend to know, under any circumstances, even one-thousandth of them. And even if it happens that a few of his faults become known to his friend, who goes and speaks of them to others - how he stands and waits, wishing the Lord to grant that they not accept his words and not believe him. And all so that he not be seen in their eyes as unworthy - even though he knows himself to be guilty of very many sins, far more than his friend has revealed. In spite of this, in the access of his self-love, everything is swept away. Thus, exactly in this way must one conduct himself vis-à-vis his friend according to the Torah, to be solicitous of his honor in every respect. And not in vain did the Torah relate to us the episode of Noach, as is written - And[46] he drank from the wine and he was inebriated and he uncovered himself

---

[45] Vayikra 19:18
[46] Bereshith 9:21-23

in the midst of his tent. And Cham the father of Canaan saw the nakedness of his father and he told his two brothers outside. And Shem and Yosef took the garment and placed it on the shoulders of both and they covered the nakedness of their father, and their faces were - kept, turned backward - when they drew near him to cover him, and the nakedness of their father they did not see. And[47] the Torah also relates to us the blessing by which Noach blessed them, and which was ultimately realized - to reveal to us the greatness of this attribute, that one must cover up any unseemliness in his friend with all of his power, just as he would for himself.

3. And sometimes he also transgresses - In[48] righteousness shall you judge your neighbor. For example, if one sees his friend saying something or doing something, which may be perceived as righteous and meritorious or as the reverse, even if he - his friend is a mediocre person, we are obligated by the Torah in this positive commandment to judge him in the scales of merit. And if that man is God-fearing, we are obligated to judge him in the scales of merit even if they incline more to guilt than to merit. And one who goes and speaks demandingly of him because of this thing that he said or that he did, or the receiver of these words, who perceives him negatively because of what he has heard about him, and does not judge him in the scales of merit, transgresses this positive commandment.

4. And if through his **Lashon Hara** [slander] or

---

[47] Bereshith 9:26-27
[48] Vayikra 19:5

Rechiluth [Gossip] he lowers his friend so that he loses his livelihood as a result, as when through evil-heartedness he publicizes his friend as being dishonest, or, if he is a worker, as being unfit for his work, or the like, he also transgresses - And[49] if your brother grows poor and his hand falls with you, then you shall uphold him - even if he be, proselyte or sojourner, and he shall live with you. And is written - And[50] your brother shall live with you. whereby we have been commanded to uphold the hand of an Israelite who has fallen **on hard times**, either by giving him a gift or a loan, or by going into partnership with him, or by finding a job for him so that he be strengthened thereby and not fall and be beholden to men. How much more so are we commanded not to cause him to lose his livelihood?

5. And sometimes, by accepting the **Lashon Hara** [slander] or the **Rechiluth** [Gossip], he also transgresses - Reprove[51] shall you reprove your neighbor. As when he sees his friend beginning to speak demandingly of another, and he knows that his words of reproof will be accepted by his friend - or even if there is a possibility that they will be accepted, the din is that he must reprove him so that the sin not be consummated. Therefore, if he allows him to consummate his **Lashon Hara** [slander], he certainly transgresses this positive commandment.

6. And all that we have written applies even if he speaks demandingly of his friend to him alone. But if he joins

---

[49] Vayikra 25:35
[50] Vayikra 25:16
[51] Vayikra 19:16

himself to a company of men of wickedness and speakers of **Lashon Hara** [slander] in order to speak to them demandingly of his friend or to hear such words from them, he transgresses also - And[52] to Him shall you cleave, which Sages explain as cleaving to Torah scholars, frequenting their assemblies in all circumstances - even eating and drinking with Torah scholars and doing business with them and joining them in all types of activities - all this, in order to learn from their deeds. Therefore, certainly, one who does the opposite of this, joining himself to a company of wicked men, transgresses this positive commandment.

7. And all this, even if not in the house of study. But if one speaks **Lashon Hara** [slander] and **Rechiluth** [Gossip] in the house of study or in the house of prayer, he also transgresses - And[53] My sanctuary shall you fear. Our house of study is included in the category of the sanctuary, as explained by the **Poskim** [Halachic Rulings]. And we have been commanded by this verse to fear the One who resides there, wherefore we may make there only reckonings of the Mitzvah, such as - those pertaining to. the Tzedakah fund and the like. How much more so is it forbidden to engage there in laughter, joking, and idle converse? And this is a categorical prohibition, as explained in **Shulchan**[54] **Aruch**. And even more so is it forbidden to speak their **Lashon Hara** [slander] or **Rechiluth** [Gossip], out of fear of the Blessed Lord who dwells there, aside from the grave **Issur** [prohibition] in

---

[52] Devarim 10:20
[53] Vayikra 19:30
[54] Orach Chayim 151:11

itself of speaking **Lashon Hara** [slander]. In speaking thus, one shows himself not to believe that the Holy One Blessed be He Reposes His **Shechina** [presence of God] in this house - Whereby he has the audacity to speak in the house of the King against the will of the King. And even those who study Torah regularly in the house of study, where they are permitted to eat and drink, as explained in the aforementioned **Shulchan**[55] **Aruch**, in any event, if they go astray in the **Issur** [prohibition] of laughing and joking or **Lashon Hara** [slander] and **Rechiluth** [Gossip] in the house of study, they transgress the positive commandment of - My sanctuary shall you fear, aside from the **Issur** [prohibition] itself. As the **Magen**[56] **Avraham on Orach Chayim** wrote - Are the Torah scholars not exhorted in respect to fear of the sanctuary? All that was permitted them, perforce, is eating and drinking because they learn in the house of study. If they had to eat and drink outside the house of study, their studies would be interrupted. As far as converse in general which is not talk of levity for Torah scholars in the house of study, see what we have written with the help of the Lord in Part Three.

8. And if the one before whom he spoke **Lashon Hara** [slander] or **Rechiluth** [Gossip] was an elder and he demeaned him with this to his face, even if he were an elderly ignoramus, he also transgresses - And[57] you shall honor the face of the elder. And even though the **Elder** of the verse refers to one who is wise, Sages have explained

---

[55] Orach Chayim 151:1
[56] Magen Avraham on Orach Chayim 151:2
[57] Vayikra 19:32

that - **And you shall honor** also reverts to - the hoary head **Seivah** [old age] that precedes it, for **honor** refers to honoring with words. That is speaking to him with honor and respect. And if he demeans him, he certainly does not honor him. Likewise, if he is wise, even if he is not elderly, he also transgresses this positive commandment. For the - **Zaken** [elder] of the verse refers to a sage, as it is expounded - **Zaken** [elder] **he who has acquired wisdom** aside from his coming many times to transgress thereby the graver **Issur** [prohibition] of shaming a Torah scholar, thereby entering the category of **Apikores** [heretic] according to the din. We shall enlarge upon this, the Lord is willing. And if he is an elder and also a sage, he transgresses - **And you shall honor** doubly.

9. And if he whom he spoke about were a Cohen, and he demeaned him thus to his face, he also transgresses - And[58] you shall sanctify him. whereby we have been exhorted to accord them - **the Cohanim** much honor. And since he speaks **Lashon Hara** [slander] or **Rechiluth** [Gossip] against him and shames him, he certainly does not honor him thereby, and he transgresses. **10.** And if he the one spoken against were his older brother, or his mother's husband or his father's wife, he also transgresses the positive commandment of **honoring**, they are having been included in this Mitzvah by the addition of - **Veeth** [and] as is written - Honor[59] your father **Veeth** [and] your mother. As explained in

---

[58] Vayikra 21:8
[59] Shemoth 20:12

Talmud[60]. How much more so - if God forbid, he speaks **Lashon Hara** [slander] against his father or mother themselves, where he certainly transgresses the positive commandment of honoring father and mother - is such **Lashon Hara** [slander] especially egregious. Aside from all this, he also transgresses - Cursed[61] is he who demeans his father and his mother. - may Heaven protect us.

11. And in all instances, he also transgresses - The[62] Lord your God shall you fear, whereby we have been exhorted to fear the Blessed Lord all the days of our life. And, when an act of transgression comes to hand, we are obligated to arouse our spirit at that time to the realization that the Holy One Blessed be He observes the deeds of all men, and **returns them vengeance** according to the evil of the deed, and in this realization, he will keep from transgressing the will of his Maker. And, of a certainty, one who abandons his soul to this grave transgression of **Lashon Hara** [slander] and **Rechiluth** [Gossip] violates this positive commandment of fearing the Lord.

12. And in all instances, he transgresses at that time of speaking **Lashon Hara** [slander] and **Rechiluth** [Gossip], the Mitzvah of learning Torah, which is an absolute positive commandment, as explained by the **Rambam**[63] and in his **Sefer**[64] **Hamitzvoth** and by all the enumerators of the mitzvoth. And there is no limit to the reward of this mitzvah, which is over and against all of

---

[60] Kethuvoth 103a
[61] Devarim 27:16
[62] Devarim 6:13
[63] Hilchoth Talmud Torah 1
[64] Positive Commandments 11

the Mitzvoth, as explained in the Mishnah[65] and in Talmud[66]. All of the Mitzvoth are not comparable to one pronouncement of the Torah. And, conversely, the punishment for its neglect is over and against all of the transgressions, as Sages have explained - The[67] Holy One Blessed be He 'overlooked' the sins of idolatry, illicit relations, and the spilling of blood; but He did not overlook the sin of neglect of Torah. At other times, one goes clean of din **on high** for the transgression of this sin of neglect of Torah study, by reason of being occupied with earning a livelihood or in pondering how to gain one. But when he speaks **Lashon Hara** [slander] or **Rechiluth** [Gossip], how does his livelihood **gain** from this? And he also transgresses in this time of speaking **Lashon Hara** [slander] many negative commandments. As explained in **Semag**[68], we have been exhorted by the Torah in many negative commandments not to separate ourselves from Torah in any manner. For there is always some way in which one can fulfill the positive commandment of studying Torah - If he is a steady learner, through his learning, and if he is not a learner, he can study the holy works that are translated into the vernacular - **Yiddish** [in our time English] in our time, such as **Chovoth Halevavoth**, **Menorath Hamaor**, and the like, and he need not remain idle from learning Torah, and speak **Lashon Hara** [slander] and **Rechiluth** [Gossip] instead. And I have also seen this idea stated in the name of the **G'RA** [the Gaon of Vilna], who explained the difference between **Din** [judgment] and **Cheshbon** [Reckoning].

---

[65] Mishna Peah 1:1
[66] Yerushalmi Peah 1:1
[67] Petichah D'Eichah Rabbati 2
[68] Negative Commandments 13

Din [judgment] - one's being judged for the transgression itself, **Cheshbon** [Reckoning] - one's being held to account - at the time of judgment for transgression - for the time he could then have spent in fulfilling a Mitzvah. Woe unto us on the day of din. What can we answer if the Holy One Blessed be He reckons against us for each moment of idle, derogatory, talk and light-headedness, or **Rechiluth** [Gossip] and **Lashon Hara** [slander] even the transgression of neglect of Torah for that time alone. For, in truth, with each word of Torah learning, one fulfills the positive commandment of Torah study itself. And if one learns a chapter of Mishnah or a page of Talmud, he fulfills many hundreds of Mitzvoth, as the GRA of blessed memory wrote in **S'hnoth**[69] **Eliyahu** in the name of the Talmud Yerushalmi. If so, the **Cheshbon** [Reckoning] comes to many thousands of holy words of Torah, each one of which is a great Mitzvah in itself, that we have actively nullified, and against them, many thousands of transgressions of neglect of the positive commandment of Torah study that we have committed at that very time! And how much more grievous is the sin if at the very time that one separates himself from Torah, he speaks **Lashon Hara** [slander] and the like? For with every demeaning remark that he makes against his friend, he transgresses a distinct negative commandment in itself, as mentioned in the Talmud[70] and in the name of **Rabbeinu Yonah** above. So that if we come to reckon only the transgression of separation from Torah for every moment of **Lashon Hara** [slander], several hundreds of transgressions of negative and positive commandments

---

[69] Peah 1:1
[70] Makkoth 20b

are added thereto. And how much more so, when we add to this the transgression of many other negative and positive commandments that we have expatiated upon until now. One must, therefore, keep himself from the recital of such vanities.

13. And all this that we have discussed until now applies even when he speaks **Lashon Hara** [slander] about his friend which is true. Still, if within his Lashon Hara [slander] or **Rechiluth** [Gossip] there becomes intermixed something which is partially false, he also transgresses a positive commandment of the Torah, as is written - From[71] a thing of falsehood keeps far. And his name Which is his classification also changes for the worse thereby, he is now called **Motzi Shem Ra** [one who spreads an evil report]. And his punishment is far more severe than that for the speaker of **Lashon Hara** [slander] and **Rechiluth** [Gossip] in general.

14. It also is apparent that in all eight modes, he also transgresses - And[72] you shall walk in His ways. Whereby we have been commanded to emulate the traits of the Holy One Blessed be He, all of which traits are for the good alone, as Sages have said in the Talmud - Just[73] as He is merciful, you, too, be merciful; just as He is gracious, you, too, be gracious, and the like with the other good traits, as is explained by the Rambam - And[74] we find with the Holy One Blessed be He, in His pure and holy traits, that He hates dilation informing in all modes,

---

[71] Shemoth 23:7
[72] Devarim 28:9
[73] Shabbath 133b
[74] Hilchoth Deoth 1:5 and 6

even against the most reprehensible of men, as Sages have said in the episode of **Achan** in the Talmud - Am[75] I the Lord a **delator**[76] for you. And He[77] hopes for the good and not for the bad. And in the Talmud[78] - Four[79] classes do not behold the Divine Presence - ...the class of the speakers of **Lashon Hara** [slander], as it is written - For[80] You are not a God who desires wickedness. Evil shall not dwell with You. Therefore, one who habituates himself to this evil trait does not walk in the way of the Lord, which is only to do good to others, and he does the opposite - wherefore the Torah designated **Lashon Hara** [slander] as **Evil** - so that he also transgresses this positive commandment That is - And you shall walk in His ways. We have thus enumerated fourteen positive commandments, which tend to be transgressed by **Lashon Hara** [slander] and **Rechiluth** [Gossip] aside from the aforementioned seventeen negative commandments. And though all the seventeen negative commandments and fourteen positive commandments cannot obtain with one man and with one slur, as is clear to the reader, still, all who are habituated, God forbid, to this evil trait will certainly transgress all of them in the course of time. For sometimes he will come to speak **Lashon Hara** [slander] against an elder, and sometimes, against a sage. And sometimes he will demean him to his face and sometimes not to his face, as mentioned above.

---

[75] Sanhedrin 11a
[76] Slander
[77] Joshua 7
[78] Sotah 42a
[79] Tanna D'bei Eliyahu 1
[80] Tehillim 5:5

Curses

And now we shall explain, with the help of the Lord, what we projected in the beginning, to detail how many **Arur** [Curses] he who does not guard himself against this evil trait beings upon himself.

1. Aside from all the aforementioned negative and positive commandments, he transgresses - Cursed[81] be he who smites his neighbor in secret, which refers to **Lashon Hara** [slander], as we find in **Sifrei** and in Rashi's commentary on Chumash.

2. He also transgresses - Cursed[82] is he who misleads the blind man on the way. It is known that the intent of Scripture is to curse one who places a stumbling block before another so that an **Issur** [prohibition] be committed by him, as in the negative commandment - And[83] before the blind man do not place a stumbling block. We have already explained[84] - As also falling into this category.

3. And if God forbid this matter becomes **Hefker** [unclaimed property] inconsequential to him, so that he does not take it upon himself to guard himself from it, he transgresses further a third **Arur** [Curse] - Cursed[85] is he who does not fulfill the words of this Torah to do them.

---

[81] Devarim 27:24
[82] Devarim 27:18
[83] Vayikra 19:14
[84] Negative Commandments 4
[85] Devarim 27:26

which is understood as his not accepting it upon himself to fulfill the entire Torah. And he is called a - **Mumar** [heretic] in respect to one thing, because of this - gratuitously transgressing this grave **Issur** [prohibition], regarding this article of the Torah of the Lord as **Hefker** [unclaimed property] - being like any other **Mumar** [heretic] in respect to the entire Torah. Therefore, his sin is too great to forgive. We have thus enumerated three **Arurin** [Curses] which are often attendant upon this evil trait.

And if God forbid, the **Lashon Hara** [slander] were against his father and mother, he also transgresses a fourth **Arur** [Curse] - Cursed[86] is he who demeans his father and his mother, which we have already explained above[87] in the **Mekor Hachaim** and in the book **Be'er Mayim Chayim**.

The following Talmud - is[88] well known - **Arur** [Curse] connotes **curse, banishment,** and **oath,** Therefore, everyone who knows himself to be remiss in this bitter sin, must fear for his soul, lest God forbid he is **banished** by Heaven because of this - as is written in Charedim regarding one who demeans his father and mother.

And yet other evils stem from the bitter sin of **Lashon Hara** [slander], such as the base trait of cruelty and that of anger, which is a grave sin, as Sages dilate upon in the Talmud - And[89] very often it leads to levity and to other evil traits of the kind. Therefore, from all the words of this introduction, from which we can understand

---

[86] Devarim 27: 16
[87] Positive Commandment 14
[88] Shevuoth 36a
[89] Shabbath 105b

the greatness of the harm wrought by **Lashon Hara** [slander] and **Rechiluth** [Gossip], the Torah has explicitly delineated this **Issur** [prohibition], assigning to it a distinct negative commandment as is written - Do[90] not go talebearing among your people. More than any of the other evil traits, as we have written at the beginning of our introduction; and the Introduction is hereby completed.

    And I would ask my friend, the reader, to constantly read and reread this introduction, for it certainly is of greater avail for the future in this regard than anything else. For it is culled from the **Rishonim** [Old Sages], whose words are pure and holy, burning like flames. And, of a certainty, they have guarded themselves from this base trait to its very end, wherefore their words make a deep impression on the hearts of their readers. And let the reader also know that I have not selected the negative and positive commandments fortuitously, but I carefully probed and expounded the 613 mitzvoth, and much did I toil until the Holy One Blessed be He helped me find those commandments relevant to our subject.

And so that it not be cause for wonder in the eyes of the reader, since the **Issur** [prohibition] of **Lashon Hara** [slander] is so great, as is that of verbal wronging, why do we find many times in the Talmud that one amora seems to be taunting his colleague. To this, too, **I opened my eyes**, and because of this, I copied the response of the **Chavoth Yair** that appears at the end of the book. And, in the book itself, I also resolved many seemingly contradictory citations, a little here, a little there.

---

[90] Vayikra 19:16

Part One

The Prohibition Against **Lashon Hara** [slander]

Principle 1

Opening Comments

In this principle, there will be explained the **Issur** [prohibition] of **Lashon Hara** [slander] - by mouth, by sign, or by letter - and the greatness of the punishment for one who is habituated to this sin, and the reward for him who guards himself from this bitter sin, and other details. It contains nine sections.

Seif 1

It is forbidden to speak demanding of one's friend, even if it be absolute truth. And this is termed everywhere by **Chazal** [Sages] **Lashon Hara** [slander]. For if there were in his words an admixture of falsehood, by which his friend is demeaned even more, this is in the category of **Motzi Shem Ra** [one who spreads an evil report], in which his sin is far greater. And the speaker of **Lashon Hara** [slander] transgresses a negative commandment, as is written - Do[1] not go talebearing among your people. And this **Lashon Hara** [slander] is also in the category of **Rechiluth** [Gossip].

Seif 2

This negative commandment that we adduced is what the

---
[1] Vayikra 19:16

Torah stated explicitly for this **Issur** [prohibition] of **Lashon Hara** [slander] and **Rechiluth** [Gossip]. But aside from this, there are many other negative and positive commandments that one transgresses by speaking **Lashon Hara** [slander], as explained above in the preceding introduction.

Seif 3

All this, only if one spoke demanding of his friend by chance. But if God forbid, he is habituated to this sin, like those who customarily sit and say - Thus and thus did **Ploni** [so and so] do. Thus, and thus did his fathers do. This and this demeaning thing did I hear about him - men such as these are called by **Chazal** [Sages] **B'aalei** [men of] **Lashon Hara** [slander] and their punishment is far greater, than that of the former. For in their perverseness of spirit and their malice of heart, they transgress the Torah of the Lord, and it becomes **Hefker** [unclaimed property] to them, as explained above in the end of the introduction. And about them, it is said in the tradition - Let[2] the Lord cut off all smooth-talking lips, the tongue that speaks haughtily.

Seif 4

Chazal [Sages] have said - For three transgressions punishment is exacted of a man in this world, and he has no share in the world to come - idolatry, illicit relations, and blood-spilling - and **Lashon Hara** [slander] over and above all. **Chazal** [Sages] have proved this from Scripture. And the **Rishonim** [the first Sages ones] have explained that the reference is to those who are habituated

---

[2] Psalms 12:4

to this sin **Lashon Hara** [slander] and who do not take it upon themselves to guard themselves against it, the thing has become **permitted** to them.

Seif 5

There is no difference in the **Issur** [prohibition] of speaking **Lashon Hara** [slander], as to whether one speaks it of his own volition or whether his friend stands over him and begs him to tell him - in either case, it is forbidden. And even if his father or his Rabbi - whom he is obligated to honor and to fear and not to contradict their words - even if they importune him to speak of a certain thing, he knows that in the midst of the account he will perforce come to speak **Lashon Hara** [slander] or even only the **Avak** [dust] of **Lashon Hara** [slander], he is forbidden to consent.

Seif 6

Even if one sees that if he takes it upon himself never to speak demanding of a Jew, or to say anything else that is forbidden, his livelihood will suffer greatly, as when he is in the employ of others who have not the faintest trace of Torah about them and it is well known that, in our many sins, such men are steeped in this sin to such an extent that if they see one whose mouth is not open in **Lashon Hara** [slander] as wide as theirs, they take him for a fool and a simpleton and because of this may dismiss him from his job and deprive him of a livelihood, in spite of this, it is forbidden to transgress, as is the case with all the other negative commandments, for[3] which one must give up all that he possesses rather than transgress.

---

[3] Yoreh Deah 157:1

Seif 7

And from this, we can understand that **Lashon Hara** [slander] is certainly forbidden in an instance where only one's personal honor is at stake. As when one is sitting in the company of men and has no way of avoiding them, and they are speaking of things which are forbidden according to the **Din** [the law]. If he sits in silence and in no way abets them in their talk, he will be regarded as **crazy**. Of this and all such things, **Chazal** [Sages] have said in the Mishna - Better[4] that a man be called **A Fool** all of his days rather than be wicked one moment before the Lord. He must harness all of his powers at that moment to withstand the trial, and if he does so, he may be completely confident that his reward for this from the Blessed Lord will be without end. As **Chazal** [Sages] has stated in the Mishna - According[5] to the strain is the reward. And, in **Avoth D'Rabbi Nathan** - One time with strain for a hundred times without strain. That is, the reward for the performance of a Mitzvah or the abstention from an **Issur** [prohibition], which entails strain, is a hundredfold more than for that of the same kind, which entails no strain. And to such a time of trial as the above there certainly applies the statement of **Chazal** [Sages] in the Midrash - For every moment that one **Muzzles** his mouth, he attains to such secreted light that no angel or Divine creature can conceive of. As to how one should conduct himself with respect to reproof and listening if one is **caught** in such an evil company as this one.

Seif 8

This **Issur** [prohibition] of **Lashon Hara** [slander] obtains whether it is actually spoken by mouth or stated

---

[4] Eduyoth 5:6
[5] Avoth 5:23

in a letter. There is also no difference whether he speaks it explicitly or by sign. In all modes, it is in the category of **Lashon Hara** [slander].

Seif 9

And know also that even if in demeaning his friend he demeaned himself with the very same slur - even if he began by railing thus against himself, he has nevertheless not left the ranks of the slanderers.

CHOFETZ Part One CHAIM

Principle 2

Opening Comments

In this principle there will be explained the **Din** [the law] of **Lashon Hara** [slander] in the presence of three ways in all its details. It contains thirteen sections.

Seif 1
It is forbidden to speak **Lashon Hara** [slander] against one's friend, even if it is true, even before one, and, more so, before many. And the more listeners, the greater the sin of the speaker, for his friend is more greatly demeaned thereby, his taint being publicized before several people. Also, in doing so, he makes several people go astray in the **Issur** [prohibition] of listening to **Lashon Hara** [slander].

Seif 2
As to there being found a **Heter** [a halachic permit] in the words of **Chazal** [Sages] to speak it before three, this applies to something which is not an absolute taint and which can be understood in two ways. It is well known that such things depend on how they are said. It is such a thing that **Chazal** [Sages] permitted to say in the presence of three, the rationale being that since he says it before three, he knows for a certainty that these things will come to the object's ears for your friend has a friend, etc. The speaker, therefore, heeds himself in speaking, so that what he says will not be understood negatively. Let one illustration serve for all cases of the same kind. If one is

asked - Where is fire found? and he answers - You can find it there, where they always cook flesh and fish. This can be understood according to how it is said at the time. If he wishes he can say it in such a tone that contains no taint against his friend. For in truth, there is sometimes no fault in this. It may be that he has a large family and that the Holy One Blessed be He has blessed him with wealth, or that he is an innkeeper or the like, and that when he the speaker is asked where the fire is to be found, he answers quite appropriately that there is no fire to be found now except in that house, where they always cook, etc. All of these things in the category of the **Avak** [dust] of **Lashon Hara** [slander] depend upon how they are expressed at the time. But if the **tone** of his voice and movements is that he the proprietor of the house or the inn, overindulges in feasting, even though this is not an absolute taint, **Chazal** [Sages] has termed it the **Avak** [dust] of **Lashon Hara** [slander], and it is forbidden to say it even in the presence of three.

Seif 3
There are some who say that if one speaks demeaningly of his friend before three, even though he certainly transgresses the **Issur** [prohibition] of **Lashon Hara** [slander], as mentioned before, still, if one of the three who heard this thing told it thereafter to others, he does not thereby transgress the **Issur** [prohibition] of **Lashon Hara** [slander], by reason of the fact that if three know of it, the thing has been heard and become known by all, for - Your friend has a friend, etc. and the Torah did not forbid as **Lashon Hara** [slander] something which is bound to be known. And this is so only if he relates it by

chance, but not if he intends to spread it and to publicize it more. Even if he does not relate it in the name of the one who told him so that there is no **Rechiluth** [Gossip], but casually, to the effect that such and such was heard about **Ploni** [so and so], still he does not escape the **Issur** [prohibition] of **Lashon Hara** [slander].

Seif 4

And even our **Heter** [a halachic permit] to repeat this to another where there is no intent to publicize it, applies only to the first hearer, who himself heard what Reuven said about Shimon in the presence of three. But he who heard it from him is forbidden to go thereafter, on the authority of his having been told that he heard it in the presence of three, and to tell another of the taint he heard attributed to Shimon, even if he does not mention who it is that purveyed this slander against Shimon - unless the thing was publicized and became known to all. And this applies not only when this second hearer does not himself know whether the allegation itself - that Reuven slandered Shimon - is true, in which instance he certainly is forbidden to believe him his informer that Reuven transgressed the **Issur** [prohibition] of **Lashon Hara** [slander]. But even if he knows himself that Reuven spoke demeaningly of Shimon, he does not know if he did so in the presence of three, in spite of this, he is forbidden to rely on his words to this effect, and we fear that perhaps it was not in the presence of three and that it is not bound to become public knowledge, wherefore he the second hearer is forbidden to tell it to anyone.

Seif 5

It seems to me that if the recounting in the presence of three were before God-fearing men, who guard themselves against the prohibitions of **Lashon Hara** [slander], then, as a matter of course, this report is not bound to be heard, and if so, it is forbidden by Torah law to repeat it afterward to another. And even if only one of the three were God-fearing, guarding himself against the **Issur** [prohibition] of **Lashon Hara** [slander], the **Din** [the law] remains the same, for there are no longer three potential **publicises**. And it may be that this is the **Din** [the law] if one of the three were a relative or a close friend of the object of the slander. The same rationale applies here. For he certainly will not go and reveal to all the taint of his relative or his close friend, so that there are not three potential **publicises** who were present.

Seif 6

It also seems to me that only in that city in which the report was heard in the presence of three is it permitted to reveal it on the basis of - Your friend has a friend, etc. But not in a different city, even if there were communication between the two caravans. See in the book **Be'er Mayim Chayim**.

Seif 7

And if the speaker exhorted the hearers not to reveal it, even if he said it before many, the **Issur** [prohibition] of **Lashon Hara** [slander] obtains for the one who reveals it afterward, even by chance. And even if he sees that one of the hearers or two did not heed this exhortation and revealed what **He** heard to others, in spite of this, this third one, may not reveal the thing to others, even by chance. See **Be'er Mayim Chayim**.

CHOFETZ CHAIM

Part One

Seif 8

There is no difference in the language of the exhortation, whether he exhorted them not to mention the subject at all anymore, or whether he said to them - Let none of this be made known by you - in all modes, it is forbidden to reveal the demeaning of another, even to a different person; how much more so to the person demeaned himself. For if it is revealed to another, in the end, it will become known to all, and even to him, the person demeaned through the channels of - Your friend has a friend, etc. It also seems obvious that the **Heter** [a halachic permit] of **Apei Telata** [the third] applies only if the hearers were three, as opposed to an instance of two who spoke before two, where this **Heter** [a halachic permit] does not apply at all. See **Be'er Mayim Chayim**.

Seif 9

And all this that we have said applies to the **Issur** [prohibition] of repeating it itself, but God forbid to add even one word or to **embroider** the thing before the hearer, as by saying that what was said against Shimon was very well said, and the like - this certainly is forbidden in all modes, for he thereby harms him with his words more than he would have been harmed had he himself heard the original report within the normal dynamics of **Apei Telata** [the third]. And, furthermore, by this adding to the original, it is clear that he accepts the report as true, and this is forbidden by all **Poskim** [Halachic Rulings] in all modes, as will be explained below, please God, see below[6]. And, therefore, one must take great heed, even if a man is known to have had a

---

[6] Principle 7, section 1

certain fault in his youth, but from then until now he has been conducting himself correctly, or if it is known about his forbears that they did not conduct themselves correctly at all, but he does not hold on to their ways, and all such things, where, in truth, he is not open to aspersion, it is forbidden to demean him or to shame him before his friends because of this early fault. And one who transgresses and speaks about these things before others, even if not in his presence, in order to shame him in the eyes of his people, even if he adds nothing to the truth, is in the class of the speakers of **Lashon Hara** [slander], who do not behold the Divine Presence, as stated in **S'haarei Teshuvah** Article 214. And the **Heter** [a halachic permit] of **Apei Telata** [the third] does not apply in such an instance, even if the thing is known to all, since, in truth, he the object of this report bears no blemish in this, as is written - The[7] son shall not bear the sin of the father. And the wicked one, when he turns from all his sins which he has done… All of the sins which he has done shall not be reckoned unto him in his righteousness. In the righteousness which he has done shall he live. And he who does bring these things up to him renders him a mockery in the mouths of men.

Seif 10

And know also that the entire **Heter** [a halachic permit] of **Apei Telata** [the third] applies to the speaker. But, as far as the hearer is concerned - that is if he knows the nature of the hearer to be such that as soon as he hears the report he will accept it as the truth against Shimon, and may even add some demeaning things against him - to a

---

[7] Yechezkel 18:20-22

man like this it is forbidden to intimate anything demeaning about his friend in any form. And one who does so **Transgresses** - Before[8] the blind man do not place a stumbling-block. as we expatiated above in the introduction in relation to this negative commandment. And all that we have written concerning this principle in the direction of **Issur** [prohibition] applies even if this speaker did not mention the name of the first speaker, who spoke in the presence of three, but only stated that this and this was heard about **Ploni** [so and so]. Even thus it is forbidden. And after all these things and this truth that we have explained, see, my brother, how much one must distance himself from this leniency of **Apei Telata** [the third], which has practically no place in reality, and, especially, even if all the conditions for leniency obtain, it is still to be determined whether the Halachah is consistent with this opinion of leniency, since, according to many **Poskim** [Halachic Rulings] there is no source for this leniency in the Talmud as we have written in section 4 in the the book **Be'er Mayim Chayim**. Therefore, one who guards his soul will distance himself from this.

Seif 11

And now, according to what we have explained, with the help of the Blessed Lord, of the principles of **Apei Telata** [the third], we realize that care must be taken that when the seven city dignitaries preside over the actions of the men of the city in matters of assessments and the like, where their judgment will be to the detriment of one and to the benefit of another, and they differ in opinion and decide according to the majority - when they leave the

---

[8] Vayikra 19:14

communal chamber, each one must take great heed not to relate thereafter his opinion or the opinion of **Ploni** [so and so] to the effect that at the beginning of the case his opinion was to be lenient with the man involved, but his colleagues overruled him and compelled him to accept their view. And it goes without saying that if they agreed among themselves from the beginning that when they left the communal chamber they would not reveal or relate their deliberations to the man involved in the debt - It goes without saying, that if he did so, this would be an absolute **Issur** [prohibition] but even if quite casually, without even intending to reveal anything, he happened to tell this to another in such a manner as to make it appear from his words that he did not incline to this the majority opinion even now, but that he could not contest it with the others, this, too, is an absolute **Issur** [prohibition]. And according to the opinion of the book **Hayad Haketanah** - Even[9] if one relates casually that it was his opinion, in the beginning, to be lenient with the man involved, it came to a vote and they decided according to the majority, this, too, is forbidden. And there is no difference between whether one reveals this of his own volition or his friend rises against him with insults over this decision which they arrived at in a certain matter. In all instances, it is forbidden to place the onus on his colleague and remove it from himself, even if what he says is true.

Seif 12

I have also found it fitting to write of another thing explicitly, for I have found many people to be habituated

---

[9] Hilchoth Deoth 9

to it. That is, when someone lectures in the house of study it is forbidden according to the **Din** [the law] to mock him and to say that there is nothing to his lectures and there is nothing to hear. And in our many sins, we see many people be remiss in this, not considering this mockery as an **Issur** [prohibition] at all. But according to the Din [the law], it is absolute **Lashon Hara** [slander]. For through such speech, it often happens that he causes monetary loss to his friend, and, sometimes, pain and shame, too. For even if it were true, **Lashon Hara** [slander] is forbidden even if true. For what benefit do this mocker and jester hope to gain by his levity? If he is a sincere person, to the contrary, he should counsel the lecturer afterward, in private, and suggest other ways to present his lecture. For in his present approach mockery, his words are not attended to, and by this the above counsel to the lecturer he would also fulfill - And[10] you shall love your neighbor as yourself. In any event, he should not render him a mockery in the mouths of men. And the **Heter** [a halachic permit] of **Apei Telata** [the third] is of no avail here as I have clearly explained in the **Be'er Mayim Chayim**.

Seif 13

If one revealed to his friend, in the presence of three, details of his occupation or trade or the like, things which, in general, are otherwise forbidden to repeat afterward to another, lest this result in injury or pain to him - now, since he himself revealed it in the presence of three, it is evident that this is of no concern to him, even if it comes to be known in the end. Therefore, the one who hears it

---

[10] Vayikra 19:18

from him is permitted ab initio to reveal it to others, so long as he - the teller does not make it clear that he is opposed to his doing so. But none of the qualifications adduced above in the discussion of **Apei Telata** [the third] should be lacking. See **Be'er Mayim Chayim**.

CHOFETZ   Part One   CHAIM

Principle 3

Opening Comments

Herein will be explained that there is no difference in the **Issur** [prohibition] of **Lashon Hara** [slander] between in his presence or not in his presence, and that the **Issur** [prohibition] of **Lashon Hara** [slander] applies even by way of jest and even if the speaker does not identify while speaking, the man that he is referring to, along with other details. It contains eight sections.

Seif 1

How great is the **Issur** [prohibition] of **Lashon Hara** [slander], which the Torah has forbidden even if true and in all modes? For not alone if he is careful to speak it only in private and to insist that it not be revealed to him, who is spoken about, is it forbidden, for through this he also brings a curse upon himself, as is written - Cursed[11] be he who smites his neighbor in secret, but even if he knows that he would speak it even to his face, or actually speaks **Lashon Hara** [slander] to his face, even so, it is forbidden and called - **Lashon Hara** [slander]. And in one respect, the **Issur** [prohibition] is greater - **To his face than not to his face**. For in his presence, aside from the **Issur** [prohibition] of **Lashon Hara** [slander], he - the speaker clothes himself with the trait of brazenness and audacity, and arouses more strife thereby. And very often this leads also to the - Whitening of the other's face in shame, as we have enlarged upon in the introduction

---
[11] Devarim 27:24

concerning the negative commandment of - Do[12] not bear sin because of him.

Seif 2

As to our sometimes finding a **Heter** [a halachic permit] in the words of **Chazal** [Sages] for him to speak as he does if he would not prevent himself from speaking thus before him, this applies only in an instance of the **Avak** [dust] of **Lashon Hara** [slander], and when he says something which may be understood in two ways so that if we explained his words in one way, there would be nothing demeaning about them. And this is known to depend upon the intent of the speaker and upon what is said at the time. For if he wishes, he can express himself by voice and movement in a very low-keyed mode, so that nothing demeaning against his friend can be detected in his words. And if he wishes, he can express himself in such a way that the listener understands his intent, in a different sense, as demeaning. And it is very difficult to determine the dividing line exactly. Therefore, **Chazal** [Sages] have said that if in the mode of movement by which he utters these words, no one would be ashamed to speak thus before his friend, it is clear that his intent is not to demean him, and it is permitted. But if it is evident from his movements that his intent is to demean him, and if so, a man, in general, would be ashamed to speak thus before his friend, even though the entire affair in itself, even if it be perceived as demeaning, is only the **Avak** [dust] of **Lashon Hara** [slander], and true, and he knows that he himself would speak thus even before him, it is nevertheless forbidden.

---

[12] Vayikra 19:17

Seif 3

And see further how great the **Issur** [prohibition] of **Lashon Hara** [slander] is. For even if he does not speak out of hatred and does not intend in what he says to demean him, but speaks only in jest and from light-headedness, still, since in truth these are demeaning words, it is forbidden by the Torah.

Seif 4

The **Issur** [prohibition] of speaking **Lashon Hara** [slander] obtains even if he does not identify, in speaking, the man that he is speaking about, but he just speaks in general terms, and from what he says the listener can understand which man he is referring to, this is in the category of **Lashon Hara** [slander]. More than this - even if there were nothing demeaning in his words themselves, but his words could cause harm or ascription of taint to his friend, which the teller intended by his deceit, this, too, is in the category of **Lashon Hara** [slander], and is called by **Chazal** [Sages] **Lashon Hara** [slander] in private.

Seif 5

And there are many other modes of Mens of **Lashon Hara** [slander] speaking by deceit. That is speaking **innocently** of their friends as if they did not know that what they spoke was **Lashon Hara** [slander], or that these were the acts of **Ploni** [so and so] his friend, etc. All such and their like are in the category of **Lashon Hara** [slander].

Seif 6

And know that even if no harm came to that man from his **Lashon Hara** [slander], as when the listeners did not accept his words or the like, even so, they do not depart from the category of **Lashon Hara** [slander] and he requires atonement. More than this - Even if he assumes from the beginning that no harm will come to him from his words, it is still forbidden to speak demeaningly of him.

Seif 7
And know further a great principle and foundation in these things - If he sees a man who did something or said something - both in the area of what is between man and his Maker or in the area of what is between man and his neighbor - and his words or his deeds can be judged in the scales of good and merit - if that man the sayer or doer is God - Fearing, he must be judged in the scales of merit, even if what he has done seems more inclined to the scales of guilt. And if he is one of the plain people, who guard themselves against sin, but occasionally stumble into it - if the doubt is balanced, he must incline it and judge him by the scales of merit, as **Chazal** [Sages] have said - If one judges his friend by the scales of merit, God will judge him by the scales of merit. And this is included in the Blessed One's behest, as stated - In[13] the scales of righteousness shall you judge your fellow. And even if the thing seems more inclined to the scales of guilt, it is very fitting that he regards it as a doubt and does not judge it in the scales of guilt. And when the thing is inclined to the scales of merit, where it is certainly forbidden, according to the **Din** [the law] to judge it in the scales of guilt, and he judges it in the scales of guilt, as a result of which he goes and demeans him - Aside from

---

[13] Vayikra 19:15

transgressing - **In righteousness shall you judge your fellow**, he transgresses further the **Issur** [prohibition] of speaking **Lashon Hara** [slander].

Seif 8

And even when the scales of guilt are more heavily weighted than those of merit, where, in respect to the din, the **Issur** [prohibition] of judging him in the scales of guilt is not so great - that is in the terms of perceiving him as not having acted in accordance with the **Din** [the law] - But he should not rush to shame him because of this before others without having ascertained that this is consistent with all of the qualifications listed below[14]. For there are many things where even though the din may not be with him, it is still forbidden to shame him because of this, as will be clear to those who study these principles.

---

[14] Principles 4 and 5 and in Principle 10

Principle 4

Opening Comments

In this principle, there will be explained the **Issur** [prohibition] of **Lashon Hara** [slander] between man and his Maker, and the **Tikkun** [correction] for this sin. It contains twelve sections.

Seif 1

It is forbidden to speak against one's friend - even if not to his face and even if it is true - something that will shame him. And not only demeaning things in general, such as mentioning about him the negative deeds of his fathers and his relatives, or his early deeds, both those between him and his Maker and those between him and his neighbor, for since he now conducts himself correctly it is forbidden to demean him with this and it is called **Lashon Hara** [slander]. But even if he saw him of late doing something unbefitting according to the **Din** [the law], one of the things between a man and his Maker for in those things between a man and his neighbor there are many distinctions, which we will explain, the Lord willing, below in Principle 10, it is also forbidden to demean him with this, even not before his face, if not following the qualifications explained below in section 7.

Seif 2

And there is no distinction in this between - Reporting him to have transgressed, an absolute negative commandment or an absolute positive commandment of the Torah, which is well known to be forbidden, in which instance he will certainly be shamed before the hearer, but even if it is something which many Jews are not careful about, in which instance he will not be greatly demeaned, such as saying about one that he does not want to learn Torah or that something which he said is false and the like unless there be some benefit in this, such as apprising his friend that something is false, intending only his benefit, as will be explained below[15] - Even in such instances, it is forbidden. For in any event, according to the speaker's words, he is a man that does not fulfill the Torah. And it is even forbidden to speak against him in the branches of the mitzvoth, such as that he is stingy and does not honor the Sabbath as he should the honoring of the Sabbath is included in the positive commandment of **Zachor** [Remember], as is written - **Zachor**[16] [Remember] the day of the Sabbath to sanctify it, as explained in Charedim. Or even if he maligns him for violating a general edict of the Rabbis, as when the Rabbis rule that ab initio this and this should not be done. And it is forbidden, even if not spoken to his face, and even if it is true, he the speaker himself, having seen him do this thing.

Seif 3

But this **Din** [the law] is subject to various qualifications, as I shall explain. For if he the object of the **Lashon Hara** [slander] were a **mediocre** person, a plain man of Israel, who generally guarded himself against sin, and **stumbled** in this sin only occasionally, it is possible to assume that

---

[15] Principle 10
[16] Shemoth 20:8

he committed this sin unintentionally, or that he did not know this thing to be forbidden, or that he thought the ruling to be a **Chumra** [stringent one], or conducing to a good trait in general, which saintly men are circumspect in - then, even if he saw him transgress this several times, he should certainly be given the benefit of the doubt, and it is forbidden to expose him so that he is not an object of shame before his people, and so that he not be shamed even in his own eyes. And it is forbidden to hate him for this, for he must be judged in the scales of merit, this being a positive commandment of the Torah, according to many **Poskim** [Halachic Rulings], as is written - In[17] the scales of righteousness shall you judge your friend.

Seif 4
But if it appeared to them[18] that the sinner knew of the **Issur** [prohibition] itself, and committed the sin intentionally - such as illicit relations, the eating of forbidden foods, or the like - the knowledge of this **Issur** [prohibition] having spread in Israel, the following must be taken into consideration - If he is **mediocre** in other things, usually guarding himself from sin, and in this sin having been seen to transgress only once and in secret, it is forbidden to reveal his sin to others, even not in his the sinner's presence, and he who does reveal it is guilty in doing so. For perhaps that sinner has repented of his evil way and his mind has been in turmoil over that sin, and he has been forgiven by the Lord. For the root of repentance is the bitterness of heart, and if he - The viewer makes this sin public. And he - The sinner, will be

---

[17] Vayikra 19:15
[18] Rabbeinu Yonah 215, 218, and 220

an object of scorn and mockery in men's eyes - after having repented of his evil and having been forgiven for his sin. Therefore, the fool, who mentions his sin, will himself be sinful and guilty. And it is not to be revealed even to the judges of the city, even if he has with him a second witness to substantiate his claim for if not, then even without this possibility of his having repented it is forbidden to reveal it, for since he is only a single witness, the judges are forbidden to believe his words and can only confirm him as - A speaker of **Lashon Hara** [slander], as we shall explain below, and there can be no benefit in his doing so - That is in revealing the sin. But he must reprove him in private for having rebelled against his God by sin, and he must tell him to take care to **fence himself off** from the factors that brought him to it so that he did not come to sin again. And his reprover must take care to speak to him gently, so as not to shame him, as it is written - Reprove[19] shall you reprove your neighbor but do not bear sin because of him in reproving him harshly. And all of this that we have written applies even if he is only a mediocre person in other respects, how much more so if he is a Torah scholar and a fearer of sin, who was suddenly overpowered by his evil inclination, in which instance it is a great sin to publicize his sin. And it is forbidden even to bethink himself of it, for it is to be assumed that he certainly repented and that though his evil inclination overpowered him once, his spirit is bitter unto him and his heart is extremely fearful within him over his guilt. As **Chazal** [Sages] have said in the Talmud - If[20] you have seen a Torah scholar who transgressed at

---

[19] Vayikra 19:17
[20] Berachoth 19a

night, do not think evil of him in the daytime, for he has certainly repented.

Seif 5

But if they see that the sinner is one of the foolish scoffers who hate their reprovers, as it is written - Do[21] not reprove the scoffer lest he hates you. And their words will certainly not be accepted, and men such as these readily return to their folly, so that he may very likely come to sin again - if so, it is better for them if they tell it to the judges of the city, so that they chastise him for his sin and keep him from future transgression. And it would seem that the same holds for telling the relatives of the sinner if we know that their words of reproof will be accepted by him[22]. And the entire intent of the teller should be for the sake of Heaven and in zeal for the Lord, and not because of their hatred of him for something else. And the judges, too, should chastise the sinner in secret and not **whiten his face** in public, as it is written - Reprove[23] shall you reprove your neighbor, but do not bear sin because of him. And all this, if they saw him with. That is if they were, two witnesses, but if he were a single witness, he may not testify against his friend, for his testimony is in vain, the judges being unable to rely upon it, as is written - One[24] witness shall not rise against a man for every transgression and for every sin. Therefore, if he does so, he is considered a **Motzi Shem Ra** [one who spreads an evil report], concerning - which our Rabbis

---

[21] Mishlei 9:8
[22] Be'er Mayim Chayim
[23] Vayikra 19:17
[24] Devarim 19:15

have said - One[25] who testified singly against his friend receives stripes of rebellion. And our sages have said - Three[26] are hated by the Holy One Blessed be He, one of them being - one who sees a thing of **Ervah** [immorality] in his friend and testifies against him singly. But he can reveal the thing secretly to the sinner's Rabbi and to his close confidant if he knows that his words will be accepted as those of two witnesses. And his Rabbi is permitted to hate him for this and to distance himself from his company until it becomes known to him that he has repented of his evil way. But his Rabbi may not tell this to others, it being no better than seeing it himself, as we have written above[27].

Seif 6
And it seems to me also that if the man were accustomed to repeat his folly, then even if his Rabbi were not very discreet so that his sin might become public knowledge, still, if his words of reproof would be accepted by the sinner so that he would no more repeat his offense, it is possible that it is permitted to reveal it to him - the Rabbi since the teller's intent is to benefit the sinner and not to demean him. And now we shall return to our previous point, that even if two saw him at the time of the sin, and he was a man who readily returned to his folly, still, it is permitted to reveal this only to the judges of the city and not to others. For, in any event, is it not true that we have seen him transgress this **Issur** [prohibition] but once? Perhaps his evil inclination overpowered him, and then

---

[25] S'haarei Teshuvah 22
[26] Pesachim 113b
[27] Section 4

he repented, groaning over this in bitterness of heart - so that this sinner has not yet left the category of **your**[28] **neighbor** because of this.

Seif 7

And all of these **Dinim** [the laws] that we have set down apply only to a man who is wont to regret his sins. But if you have probed his ways and seen that the fear of God is not before his eyes and that he always persists in a way that is not good - such as one who divests himself of the yoke of Heaven or is unheedful of a transgression which every one of his people knows to be a transgression - that is, whether the sin you wish to reveal has been committed deliberately many times by the sinner or he often transgresses deliberately a different sin which is known by all to be a sin - then it is apparent that it is not because his evil inclination overpowered him that he transgressed the word of the Lord, but that he does as his heart sees fit and the fear of God is not before his eyes. Therefore, it is permitted to shame him and to speak demeaningly of him, both before him and in his absence. And if he does something or says something which can be judged either in the scales of merit or in the scales of guilt, he must be judged in the scales of guilt, since he has shown himself to be an absolute evildoer in his other affairs. And thus have our Rabbis in the Talmud said - And[29] you shall not wrong, one man, his **Amito** [fellow] as is written - A[30] people who is with **Amito** [fellow] - in Torah and Mitzvoth do not wrong him with words. And if one does

---

[28] see Vayikra 19:17
[29] Bava Metzia 59a
[30] Vayikra 25:17

not direct his heart to the word of the Lord, it is permitted to shame him for his deeds, to make known his abominations, and to spill scorn upon him. And they said further in The Talmud - Flatterers[31] are exposed because of the desecration of the Name that they engender. And much more so if one reproved him for his sin and he did not desist from it, is it permitted to expose him and to reveal his sin in **the public gate** and to spill scorn upon him, until he returns to the good, as the Rambam[32] has written. But it is important not to forget certain considerations that this entails, which I have written of in the book **Be'er Mayim Chayim**.

Seif 8

When **Beth-Din** [Court] tells a man a certain **Din** [the law] involving a positive commandment, whether in the area of **between man and his Maker** or in that of **between man and his neighbor**, and he absolutely refuses to fulfill it and has no rationale for his refusal, it is permitted to speak demeaningly of him and even to record his refractoriness in the registry for all the generations to see. And if he attempts to excuse his behavior, his **Din** [the law] is as follows - If we understand that what he says is not true, but merely an attempt to push us off, we need not believe him, and we may demean him and even record his taint, as mentioned above. But if there is some doubt, it is forbidden to speak demeaningly of him.

Seif 9

And now we return to what we began with. From what we wrote in the beginning, we learn that it is forbidden to

---

[31] Yoma 86b
[32] Hilchoth Deoth 6:8

demean one's friend and to tell of his negative traits, as when we see him to be haughty or to become inordinately angry or to display other unsightly traits, which That is the possession of which traits is absolutely degrading. And though it is true that he did act as related of him, who knows if he did not repent in bitterness of heart over these evil traits? And even if one saw that he was habituated to these evil traits and that he was not bitter over them at all - in spite of this, it is forbidden to berate him. For perhaps he is unaware of the gravity of the **Issur** [prohibition]. For, in truth, we see it patently in many individuals, even sometimes in Torah scholars, that they do not regard these evil traits as such a grave **Issur** [prohibition] - as they are, indeed, in truth, to those who contemplate them in Scripture and in the words of **Chazal** [Sages] - but only as something not quite appropriate. And perhaps this sinner, too, is of this mind. And if he knew the true gravity of the **Issur** [prohibition], it is possible that he would exert all of his powers not to transgress them - As it says in Talmud - If[33] he the sinner were **Shogeg** [unwitting] relative to **Kareth** [cutting-off]. That is if he did not know that the sin were punishable by the grave penalty of **Kareth** [cutting-off], and he were **witting** relative to having transgressed a negative commandment, his act is called **unwitting** in that he is not aware of its full gravity. On the contrary, if one sees that the sinner is habituated to one of these evil traits, he should reprove him and impress upon him the gravity of the **Issur** [prohibition]. And in this, he would be fulfilling the positive commandment of - **Reprove shall you reprove your fellow**. And it is possible that he would admit that

---

[33] Shabbath 69a

he was doing wrong, but that at the time his way was just in his eyes, as is written - A[34] man's every way is just in his eyes. Therefore, it is forbidden to perceive him as **wicked** and to go and speak demeaningly of him.

Seif 10

And even so, if one sees a degrading trait in a person, such as haughtiness or anger or other evil traits or that he neglects Torah study and the like, it is proper for him to tell this to his son or to his students, and to exhort them not to keep company with him so as not to learn from his deeds. For the root of the Torah's exhortation against **Lashon Hara** [slander], even when what is said is true, applies when one's intent is to shame his friend and to rejoice in his shame. But if his intent is to guard his friend against learning from his sinner's ways, it is obviously permitted and is also accounted for as a Mitzvah. Yet, in this case, and the like, it seems that it is a Mitzvah for the teller to explain the reason that he is speaking demeaningly of his friend so that the listener does not err in permitting through him the speaker even more leniency than this, and also so that he the listener not come to wonder how he the speaker can thus contradict himself. For at one time, he tells him that it is forbidden to speak **Lashon Hara** [slander] even if it is true as will be explained below[35], that it is a great Mitzvah to separate one's young children from this sin, and now, he himself speaks it. A parallel can be found in **Shulchan**[36] **Aruch**, as to whether on Sabbath eve certain things may be

---

[34] Mishlei 21:2
[35] Principle 9
[36] Shulchan Aruch, Yoreh Deah 242

permitted, which other **Poskim** [Halachic Rulings] forbid, and the like.

Seif 11

And note also a great fundamental in these things - If one wishes to bring his friend into his affairs, such as to hire him for his work or to go into partnership with him or to make a match with him, and the like, even if until now he has heard nothing negative about him, still, it is permitted to make inquiries of people as to his character and his dealings. Even though they may tell him something negative about him, still it is permitted, since his intent is for his own good alone, so that he will not come afterward to injury or to strife or to contention and desecration of the Name, God forbid. But it appears to me that he must apprise the one he is making inquiry of, that he wishes to make a match with him, the one he is inquiring about, or enter some kind of partnership, as mentioned above. If he does so, there will be no fear of **Issur** [prohibition] - neither because of his questions, because he has no desire to demean him, but desires only his own benefit, as we have explained - though he must take care not to believe his answer completely if negative by virtue of the **Issur** [prohibition] of accepting **Lashon Hara** [slander], but he must **hear** the answer by way of suspicion only - to protect himself - nor is there any **Issur** [prohibition] by virtue of the answer of his neighbor that would cause us to say that he the inquirer transgresses - Before[37] the blind man you shall not place a stumbling block. For even if he the answerer speaks about him the one inquired about completely pejoratively, he, too, is not guilty of any **Issur**

---

[37] Leviticus 19:14

[prohibition] thereby, since his intent, too, is not to speak demeaningly of his friend, but to tell the truth in order to benefit this inquirer, who has taken counsel with him in this affair, as we explained elsewhere, this being permitted by the **Din** [the law]. But he the answerer must take great care not to exaggerate his response beyond what he knows to be the truth of the matter and beyond furnishing other details pertinent to the inquiry see below[38], of **Hilchoth** [the lows] of **Rechiluth** [Gossip] in this connection. But if he does not apprise his friend of the reason for his inquiry, but makes himself **as a stranger** to the subject of his inquiry so that he comes to know better the character of that man inquired about, it seems obvious that he will be in transgression of - Before a blind man, etc. For through him his friend the answerer will perform an **Issur** [prohibition] if he speaks derogatory things about him, even if they be true, as we have explained elsewhere. For the **Issur** [prohibition] of **Lashon Hara** [slander] applies even to what is true, according to all of the **Poskim** [Halachic Rulings]. And it may not be spoken unless he intends that in speaking thus demandingly of him some goodwill **sprout** for another. But this lacking, he may not speak it. And even if through his speaking it some good does redound to another, still, his intent was to demean. Therefore, he the inquirer must do as we have written.

Seif 12
And if he transgressed and spoke **Lashon Hara** [slander] about his friend and came to repent, it his repentance depends upon this: If his friends rejected his words and

---
[38] Principle 9

his friend was in no way demeaned by this **Lashon Hara** [slander] in their eyes, if so, there adheres to him only the sin of **between man and his Maker** and not that of between **man and his neighbor**, his having transgressed the will of the Lord, who commanded this that **Lashon Hara** [slander] must not be spoken, as we wrote above in the introduction. His correction is to regret what has passed, confess his sin, and take it upon himself with a full heart not to repeat this sin in the future, as with all sins between man and his Maker. But if his friend were demeaned by this in the eyes of the hearers and through this suffered physical or financial harm, or if he were caused emotional pain by this, this is in the category of all the sins between man and his neighbor, which even **Yom Kippur** and the day of death do not atone for until he conciliates his neighbor. He must, therefore, ask pardon of his friend for this, and when he is conciliated and forgives him, there remains with him only the sin of between man and his Maker, and he must do as mentioned above. And even if his friend does not yet know anything about it, he must reveal what he did to him which was not in accordance with the **Din** [the law], and ask forgiveness of him for this, since he knows that through him this harm was done him. From this, we can understand how much one must take care to guard himself from this pernicious trait of **Lashon Hara** [slander], for if one is steeped in this, God forbid, teshuvah repentance is almost impossible for him. For he certainly will not remember all of the souls whom he grieved by this **Lashon Hara** [slander]. And even those people whom he remembers as having stirred up evil against will not know of it, wherefore he will be ashamed to reveal it to them. And sometimes 54 he will speak of a family taint and thereby harm all the future generations so that he can never be pardoned for this. As **Chazal** [Sages] have said in the Talmud - One[39] who speaks of a family taint never has atonement for this. Therefore, one must distance himself from this extremely pernicious trait, so that he not thereafter be, God forbid, in the category of - The[40] crooked cannot be straightened.

---

[39] Yerushalmi Bava Kamma 8:7
[40] Koheleth 1:15

CHOFETZ CHAIM

Part One

Principle 5

Opening Comments

This principle there will be explained as part of the **Issur** [prohibition] of **Lashon Hara** [slander] in matters - between man and his neighbor - the question of the negation of good attributes, the **Dinim** [the laws] of **Lashon Hara** [slander] that are dependent upon the man spoken of, and the **Issur** [prohibition] of **Lashon Hara** [slander] about the property of one's friend. It contains eight sections.

Seif 1

Just as it is forbidden to shame one's friend in matters between man and his Maker, so is it forbidden to shame him in matters between man and his neighbor, even if what is said contains no admixture of falsehood. And I will not **conceal under my tongue** that there are in this principle many roots and branches, and that often this **Din** [the law] changes with the circumstances. We shall speak about this at length, God willing, below[41]. But now we shall discuss one element that is forbidden beyond a doubt. That is if one sees another asking his friend to lend him money even though this - That is to lend is a positive commandment of the Torah - When[42] you lend money, etc. As explained in the Book[43] of the Mitzvoth of the Rambam, or asking him for some other favor, which he

---

[41] Principle 10
[42] Shemoth 22:24
[43] Positive Commandments 197

does not grant him, or if he sees one transgressing negative commandment between man and his neighbor, such as taking revenge and bearing a grudge, as is explained in Talmud - Which[44] is revenge and which is bearing a grudge, etc.? - Since he the object of the **Lashon Hara** [slander] did not do him - the speaker any evil and there is also no benefit accruing to the affected party by his - the speaker recounting this to others, therefore, if he goes and recounts this to others, it is called - **Lashon Hara** [slander] according to the **Din** [the law]. And all this, even if it happened to - the speaker himself, and it was also clear to him that he could have done him this favor, but refused to do so out of the perverseness of his nature. And there obtain here also all the elements of the **Issur** [prohibition] which were explained in the preceding principle in section 3 concerning **between man and his Maker**. And even if the withholding of the favor was to another, and the speaker's intent was only zeal for the truth how much more so if the withholding of the favor were to the speaker himself, it is certainly forbidden thereafter, to go and demean him for this. And one who transgresses this, aside from stumbling into the sin of **Lashon Hara** [slander], also stumbles in this into the transgression is written - You[45] shall not bear a grudge. And if he intends by what he says to take revenge of him for this, and to publicize the other's perverseness, he transgresses in addition - You[46] shall not take revenge. Aside from the **Issur** [prohibition] of **Lashon Hara** [slander].

---

[44] Yoma 23a
[45] Vayikra 19:18
[46] Vayikra 19:18

Seif 2

Now up to this point, we have discussed many areas of forbidden speech which sometimes change in **Din** [the law] That is forbidden or permitted according to the circumstances. And now in these sections, we shall speak of the greater part of its components, where there is nothing to say on behalf of the speaker, when he intends no benefit, but only to speak demeaningly of his friend. The stumbling block here is more prevalent, almost everybody stumbling into it - and only because of insufficiency of knowledge. I shall, therefore, ask that it not be cause for wonder in the eyes of the reader that I expatiate upon it and mention every detail explicitly. For I venture to think that perhaps the Lord will grant that through this, part of this great stumbling block will be removed. And I shall begin by saying that it is forbidden to shame one's friend for insufficiency in what he possesses - whether in wisdom, strength, wealth, or the like. I shall explain my meaning in all of its details - **Wisdom** - telling people that **Ploni** [so and so] is not wise. And there is no difference here as to whether it is false or partially true and he exaggerates the actuality. This is certainly a great sin, in the order of **spreading an evil report**. For he demeans his friend by his falsehoods. - But even if it is the absolute truth, have not all the **Rishonim** [the first Sages ones] - Rooted it within us that **Lashon Hara** [slander] is forbidden even if true. And this thing, negating one's possession of a certain eminence, is certainly also in the category of **Lashon Hara** [slander]. For did the Rambam not write - **Lashon**[47] **Hara** [slander] is relating one's evils and his blemishes and demeaning a

---

[47] Rambam on Avoth 1:17

Jew in any way, even if the demeaned one were indeed deficient, etc. As he expatiates there, it is called **Lashon Hara** [slander] if what he says about him is true. See also what the Rambam has written in Hilchoth Deoth[48] to the effect that **Lashon Hara** [slander] is something, which when it becomes known to men, causes someone to be harmed in his body or in his money or to aggrieve him or to frighten him. It seems clear, then, that negating one's possession of a certain eminence is absolute **Lashon Hara** [slander] according to the Torah. Upon reflection, we find that this can result in monetary loss or grief, etc. First, we shall explain what we are dealing with now, one's saying about another that he is not wise. For, in truth, there is no attribution of deficiency greater than this. For if he were not yet married, if this **Lashon Hara** [slander] were known to people, no one would be found who would want to make a match with him. And if he had an occupation, then whatever occupation he had, whether he was a craftsman or a teacher, who would want to join him in his affairs? And especially if he were a teacher of Law in Israel - That is a posek, and one said about him to people that he was not wise, then aside from this being an **Issur** [prohibition] of **Lashon Hara** [slander] according to the Torah for certainly, if this were accepted by the hearers and publicized in the city, he would be caused a monetary loss, for no one would want to go to him for **Din** [the law] or **Pesharah** [compromise], aside from this, even something worse could happen - that by being demeaned before the men of the city, he would, in the end, be removed from his place, and his blood and the blood of his children would be on the head of the speaker;

---

[48] Rambam Hilchoth Deoth 7:5

for through his **Lashon Hara** [slander], he would have descended to the taking of his very livelihood. In addition to this, he greatly demeans thereby the honor of the Torah and its learners and is called - **The shamer of a Torah scholar**, about which **Chazal** [Sages] have said in the Talmud - There[49] is no healing for his wound. And through this **Lashon Hara** [slander] there will greatly decline the fulfillment of Torah, for if the Rabbi exhorts them thereafter concerning a certain Mitzvah in the Torah, they will pay no attention to his words, his having already been publicized in their eyes by the men of **Lashon Hara** [slander] as a man who is not wise.

Seif 3
Further, I will ask you, my brother, about the wiles of the evil inclination for my asking you this, which is not in the category of **Lashon Hara** [slander]. Look into yourself - If it were known to you of a certainty that one publicized about you that you were not wise and the like in the area of negation of eminence, how resentful you would be of him for this! You would think - What signs of folly did he see in me? He is nothing other than an evil-hearted person and a speaker of **Lashon Hara** [slander], whose desire is only to demean his friend and degrade him. And yet, when you yourself do this to your friend, who in many things is much better than you to the Lord and to people, you do not see this as a sin at all. See the great blindness in this. And, in truth, when you reflect upon this, you will find in this instance of the varieties of the **Issur** [prohibition] of **Lashon Hara** [slander] many more elements than in the others. This is so because in other

---

[49] Shabbat 119:2

instances of his saying about his friend that he transgressed an **Issur** [prohibition] both in the area of **between man and his Maker** or in the area of **between man and his neighbor**, it very often happens that his sole intent is zeal for the Lord. And though this is of no avail for the **Din** [the law] it is still being considered **Lashon**[50] **Hara** [slander] still his intent was not for evil, as opposed to this instance, where his sole intent was to demean his friend and degrade him, an egregiously bad trait, as explained in the book **S'haarei Teshuvah** of Rabbeinu Yonah. And also, in terms of the hearer. For in the other aforementioned instances of **Lashon Hara** [slander], his, the speaker's words are not immediately accepted. And, of certainty, many listeners will say - So long as we do not see it with our own eyes, we will not believe it. And certainly, in what you have said, even if it is true, there must have been some mitigating circumstances which led him to act in this manner, for, as it was told, we cannot believe such things of him. And if it develops afterward that what he said is false, the speaker will be an object of scorn and shame to all, for having spread a false report of his friend. But in this instance, if he degrades his friend and publicizes him as a fool and a simpleton to all, as a result of which all the townspeople will make him an object of shame and scorn, it often happens, in our many sins, that not one of the hearers will say - Speak less and pity the honor of Israel. Why do you have to shame him so much - As if the speaker had done no wrong thereby? And of such a speaker it is said - She[51] ate and wiped her mouth and said I have done no wrong.

---

[50] Principle 4, section 2, and also section 1
[51] Mishlei 30:20

Seif 4

And all that we have written applies even if he said about him only that he is not wise in worldly matters. How much more so, if he said about one whom the people of the city thought to be wise in Torah, that he is not so wise, and that he knows but little in Torah, and through this they come to think less of him. Certainly, this is in the category of **Lashon Hara** [slander], even if true, since his intent is not for benefit but only to lower his friend in the esteem of the hearers. For through this, on whichever level he stands, this can cause him harm, or, in any event, distress. I will provide two illustrations. If one says about the city Rabbi before the people of the city that he is not very wise in Torah, but that he knows a little of the halachic rulings that are needed in practice - even if this be true, it is absolute **Lashon Hara** [slander] according to the Torah. For by this, he completely lowers his honor and undermines his very livelihood, and decreases thereby the honor of the Torah and the fulfillment of its mitzvoth as mentioned in section 2. The same applies if he says the like about one who was recently married in the city. For certainly his honor will fall in the end in the eyes of his in laws and of the members of his household when it becomes known to them that he is of little consequence in the city. And there is no greater harm and pain than this and the like. It is difficult for me to illustrate everything, as is written - Give[52] to the wise and he will wax yet wiser. For I have come only to arouse, and the wise man will understand all by himself. And know also that the same applies if he says about a worker that he is not a good worker. This, too, is absolute **Lashon Hara**

---

[52] Mishlei 9:9

CHOFETZ   Part One   CHAIM

[slander], for here, too, all the aforementioned considerations apply. And if in this and all the other instances that we have spoken of, his intent is not to demean, but only to derive some benefit, this will be discussed, the Lord willing, in Principle 9 of the laws of **Rechiluth** [Gossip].

Seif 5

And now we shall explain what we wrote above[53] about demeaning one **in respect to strength**. That is, to say about one before the men of the city that he is by nature a weak man. That is, the **Din** [the law] in this case depends upon the circumstances. If, according to the circumstances, he can be harmed by this, as when he is a day laborer or a teacher and there are many of this kind, then certainly what he says is in the category of **Lashon Hara** [slander]. And, **in respect to wealth**. That is, to say about one before others that he is poor or not wealthy - As they say about him in the city - And that whatever he has is on credit to others. This, too, is in the category of **Lashon Hara** [slander]. Certainly, if this becomes public knowledge, he will not thereafter find anyone to extend him credit, and this will cause him harm and great distress, and it will threaten his very livelihood. And, overall, the man of heart must certainly take care if he intends no particular benefit, that there not result from this any harm to the one spoken about. And if, in all of these instances, he must say what he does in anticipation of some benefit, all of this will be treated below That is, in which circumstances and by what means, the Lord willing[54]. And one must take great care not to be hasty to be lenient in this matter and say - I do not intend to demean this man but to

---

[53] Section 2
[54] Book 2, Principle 9

derive such and such benefit. For there are many details that must first be resolved.

Seif 6

And now also a basic principle concerning **Lashon Hara** [slander] - that it depends upon the man spoken of. So that it is quite possible for one to say the same thing about two people and to be praising the one and speaking **Lashon Hara** [slander] of the other. For example, if he says about someone, whose sustenance is provided by others and who has no problems with a livelihood, that he learns Torah about three or four hours a day, he would be demeaning him greatly and would be guilty of **Lashon Hara** [slander]. But if he said the very same thing about one who toils for a living, this would be great praise. And the same applies to other instances of positive commandments, such as that of honoring the Sabbath. So that if he said about one of the poor townsmen that he spends this and this a substantial sum for him to honor the holy Sabbath, this is great praise for him. But if he said the very same thing about one who was considered a wealthy man, it would be very demeaning to him, and he would be scorned by men because of this, and he - the speaker would be guilty of **Lashon Hara** [slander]. The same applies to the giving of charity. That is, whether or not it is **Lashon Hara** [slander] depends upon the object's financial status. What is praise to one, is an insult to the other. And thus, with Mitzvoth between man and his neighbor. If it is said about a mediocre person that he conducts himself in such and such a manner with his employees, it would not be demeaning to him. But if the very same thing is said about a man of eminence in Israel,

CHOFETZ   Part One   CHAIM

it would be demeaning to him and thus in all similar instances. Therefore, it is very difficult to include in a book all of the instances in which one can fall prey to **Lashon Hara** [slander]. But make the words of the Rambam[55] - **a crown to your head**, and remember them always - That anything which, when publicized, can cause his friend physical harm, or monetary loss, or pain, or fright is **Lashon Hara** [slander]. And take care, my brother, that the evil inclination does not deceive you into saying - But have **Chazal** [Sages] not said in the Talmud - Whatever[56] is hateful to you, do not do to your friend? What have I said about him? That he learns Torah only three or four hours a day? Am I commanded to love him more than I love myself? Would that they said about me that I learned Torah three or four hours a day. And the same with charity, Sabbath expenses, and the like. In truth, this is a mistake, for the intent of the Talmud - **All**[57] **that is hateful to you** is **All that would be hateful to you if you were on his level**. And, in truth, this is dependent upon the person that is spoken of, and the place and the time. If under the circumstances this - That is, what you say about him would be demeaning to him, this certainly is **Lashon Hara** [slander] according to the **Din** [the law].

Seif 7

And know that just as it is forbidden to slander one's friend, so is it forbidden to **slander** his possessions[58]. And it is very common, in our many sins, that one shopkeeper

---

[55] Hilchot Deoth 7
[56] Shabbath 31b
[57] Shabbath 31b
[58] See Rabbeinu Eliezer Mimitz in Sefer Yere'im

slanders the wares of another, and so, in other instances of the same kind, out of envy. And this is absolute **Lashon Hara** [slander] according to the Torah.

Seif 8

The **Issur** [prohibition] of speaking **Lashon Hara** [slander], which the Torah forbade in speaking demeaningly of one's friend, applies even if it be true, and even in private; how much more so is it forbidden to speak demeaningly of one's friend before two. The sin is greater than doing so before one, for people will more readily believe it, and he will be more greatly scorned in their eyes if they hear it from two. And whenever the **Issur** [prohibition] of **Lashon Hara** [slander] is mentioned in general, the intent is in all eight modes, unless we indicate otherwise.

CHOFETZ CHAIM
Part One

Principle 6

Opening Comments

In this principle there will be explained the **Issur** [prohibition] of accepting **Lashon Hara** [slander] and hearing **Lashon Hara** [slander], and how one should conduct himself in this matter ab initio, and also, if he is **caught** in a bad company of **men of the tongue**, how he should conduct himself in accordance with the Torah, and many other details. It contains twelve sections.

Seif 1

It is forbidden to accept **Lashon Hara** [slander] according to the Torah, both in things **between man and his Maker** and things **between man and his neighbor**. That is, we may not believe in our hearts that what is said is true. For, if we do, we will look down upon the one spoken of. And this applies even if he - the hearer, explicitly disagrees with what is said. For if not, he doubles the sin - speaking by being an accessory to the speaker - and accepting. And the accepter transgresses is written - You[59] shall not bear a false report. concerning which **Chazal** [Sages] has said in the **Mechilta**, that this is an exhortation against accepting **Lashon Hara** [slander], aside from the other negative commandments and positive commandments adjoined to this, as we have written in the introduction. And **Chazal** [Sages] have said in the Talmud - That[60] all who accept **Lashon Hara**

---
[59] Shemoth 23:1
[60] Pesachim 118a

[slander] deserve to be cast to the dogs. It is written -You[61] shall not bear a false report, preceded by - To[62] the dog shall you cast it. And they have also said the Rambam[63] - The punishment of the accepter is greater than that of the teller.

Seif 2
Even on hearing **Lashon Hara** [slander] alone, there is an **Issur** [prohibition] according to the Torah even if at the time of the hearing he does not intend to accept what is said since he inclines his ear to hear. But there is a difference between hearing and accepting in several respects. For in hearing alone, without accepting, there is no **Issur** [prohibition] only when what is said does not affect him in the future. But if it does if true, as when he understands from the beginning of what he says that he wishes to show that the one spoken about is not to be trusted, and the like - if, originally, he - the hearer, intended to take him into his business or to enter into partnership with him or to make a match with him, and the like, he is permitted ab initio to listen and to suspect that it might be true so that he can guard himself against him. This is permitted since his intent is not to listen to the demeaning of his friend, but to guard himself against future injury or strife and contention and the like. The same applies when he derives no personal benefit from what is said, but if by his listening, some benefit may result for others, it is also permitted. As when he wishes to hear this thing in order to find out afterward if it is true

---

[61] Shemoth 23:1
[62] Shemoth 22:30
[63] Hilchoth Deoth 7:13

and to reprove him - who is spoken about, for this. Perhaps this will result in the sinner's repenting, or in returning the theft to its owners, or to appease the one he **insulted and blasphemed**, and the like, in which instance it is permitted. But to accept it - that is, to believe in his heart that it is true - is forbidden in all instances.

Seif 3

And let it not be cause for wonder in the eyes of the reader - If so, how can we satisfy the demands of Heaven - That is - **between man and his Maker**, if you have fenced the way against us, that even the hearing alone of one's friend being demeaned is forbidden - Perhaps it might affect me in my business or the like? The answer - If one wishes to satisfy the demands of Heaven vis-a-vis hearing, let him deport himself thus - If one comes to him and wishes to tell him about his friend, and he understands that he wishes to say something demeaning about him, let him ask at the outset - What you want to tell me, might it affect me in the future, or might I by hearing it be able to correct things by reproof, or the like? If he answers him in the affirmative, he is permitted to hear it. And he may not believe it as of yet, but only suspect, until the thing is probed. But if he understands from his answer that no benefit will be derived by the hearing, or that the speaker only wishes to vent his wrath against the one spoken about by acrimoniously imputing evil to him in the greatness of his hatred of him, it is forbidden even to hear.

Seif 4

And sometimes it is a Mitzvah to hear one's speaking demeaningly of his friend, as when he feels that by hearing the story completely, he might be able thereafter to show the speaker or the other listeners that what was said about him was not true, or other things in his favor. And there are yet other circumstances in which it is a Mitzvah to hear. As when one comes before him to complain against his friend for something he has done against him, and he knows that by listening to him he might assuage his wrath so that he will not repeat the story to others, for perhaps the others would believe him and thereby be accepters of **Lashon Hara** [slander], and by this, he would **increase peace in Israel**. But in all of the **Heterim** [a halachic permit] that we have mentioned in respect to hearing, he must take great care not to believe what he hears categorically, but only to **suspect**, so that he, too, not be ensnared in the net of the acceptance of **Lashon Hara** [slander].

Seif 5

And now let us return to our subject. Our having written[64] that even hearing **Lashon Hara** [slander] is an **Issur** [prohibition] of the Torah - that is, to go and hear. But if one was sitting in the company of people who had gathered for a certain purpose, and they began to speak forbidden things, and he feels that his words of reproof would be of no avail to them, what he should do depends upon the following - If[65] it is possible for him to leave them or to place his fingers in his ears, it is a great Mitzvah for him to do so, as **Chazal** [Sages] says in the Talmud. But if it is impossible for him to leave, and he feels that this device of putting his fingers in his ears is

---

[64] in section 2
[65] Kethuvoth 5a

also very difficult for him for they would mock him and he certainly could not do this, in any event, let him see to it to gird himself at this time of trial, and **battle the war of the Lord with his evil inclination**, not to stumble, in any event, into the **Issur** [prohibition] of the Torah of hearing and accepting **Lashon Hara** [slander]. This entails three requirements of which he must take great heed so that he rescues himself from the **Issur** [prohibition] of the Torah which inheres in this sin -

> **A.** He must resolve within himself with a firm resolve, not to believe the demeaning things they say about their friends.
> **B.** He should not be **comfortable** in hearing these forbidden things.
> **C.** He must discipline himself not to reveal to the speakers any movement from which it would appear that he agrees with what they are saying.

Seif 6

When does the foregoing apply? When at the time he sat down among them they were not engaged in forbidden speech, and even now, he cannot get away from them. But if at the time that he wanted to sit among them, they had already begun to speak in this manner, or if he could have gotten away from them and he was lax in doing so, or if he knew these men to be **natural slanderers**, whose desire was always to speak demeaningly of their friends, and he went and sat among them - even though he took no part in their conversation and was **uncomfortable** with them, still he is called a **Poshea** [offender], like them, for having transgressed the words of **Chazal** [Sages], who commanded that one distance himself from improper words. How much more so if his intent is to hear their words? His sin is **too great to bear**, and he will be inscribed because of this, above, in the **Book of Remembrances** as a wicked man and - a man of **Lashon Hara** [slander], as we find in **Pirkei D'Rabbi Eliezer**, in the will of Rabbi Eliezer Hagadol to his son Hyrkanus - My son, do not sit in the company of those who speak ill of their friends. For when their words rise above, they are written in a book. And all who stand there are written down as a company of wickedness and men of **Lashon Hara** [slander]. Therefore, men must greatly distance themselves from an evil company such as this.

Seif 7

And know that just as we have written in the name of the **Poskim** [Halachic Rulings] that according to the Torah, it is forbidden to believe demeaning things that others say about their friends, so the **Din** [the law] is that even if one knows that what was told him is true, but that they could incline his judgment in one direction or another, and the one who told him judged him in the scales of guilt, wherefore he demeaned him - and it is known that it is a Mitzvah for the hearer to judge him in the scales of merit, and this is a **Din** [the law] in the Talmud[66] and a positive commandment of the Torah according to several **Poskim** [Halachic Rulings] - and if one transgresses this and does not judge him in the scales of merit, and agrees with the speaker, who demeans him - not only does he transgress - In[67] righteousness shall you judge your neighbor. but he is also called - an accepter of **Lashon Hara** [slander].

---

[66] Shevuoth 30a
[67] Vayikra 19:15

Because he did not judge him on the scales of merit, the demeaning words came to be believed of him.

Seif 8

And all this even if the story were about a plain man, who usually was careful not to sin, but sometimes stumbled into it. How much more so if it were about a God-fearing man, to whom there applies, even more, the Mitzvah of - In[68] righteousness shall you judge your neighbor. see the Rambam[69]. And he - the hearer transgresses this and judges him in the scales of guilt, agreeing with the speaker in his demeaning of him! Of a certainty, he transgresses the **Issur** [prohibition] of accepting **Lashon Hara** [slander].

Seif 9

Just as the **Issur** [prohibition] of accepting **Lashon Hara** [slander] obtains when the speaker says about someone that he now did something improper, concerning which we were commanded not to believe in our heart that the story is true as mentioned above[70], so does it obtain relative to the other instances of the **Issur** [prohibition] of speaking **Lashon Hara** [slander] that we explained above such as shaming one with the deeds of his forbears or with his own early misdeeds, since he now conducts himself correctly, or shaming him with a lack of wisdom, both in Torah and in worldly affairs, and the like as mentioned above[71]. In anything that is demeaning to him, we have been commanded, likewise, not to accept the words of the

---

[68] Vayikra 19:15
[69] Rambam on Avoth 1:6, Rabbeinu Yonah, S'haarei Teshuvah 218
[70] section 1
[71] Principle 4 and 5

speaker for the one spoken of to be shamed in our eyes. In sum: Wherever there is an **Issur** [prohibition] vis-à-vis the speaker for his speaking, there is an **Issur** [prohibition] vis-à-vis the accepter for his acceptance.

Seif 10
Even though we explained that acceptance of **Lashon Hara** [slander] - that is, to believe in one's heart that the thing is true - is forbidden according to the Torah, still, **Chazal** [Sages] have said in the Talmud - One[72] must nevertheless, suspect. That is, one must accept the thing on the level of suspicion alone, to guard himself from him the object of the **Lashon Hara** [slander] so that no harm comes to him at his hand. And let there be no doubt about the fact that a man is assumed to be kosher - unless proven otherwise. And so, he - the hearer is still obligated to grant him the one spoken about all the good commanded by the Torah - to be accorded to all the men of Israel. For his worth has not been diminished in our eyes in any way because of this **Lashon Hara** [slander]. But the Torah has allowed us to be suspicious on the basis of the **Lashon Hara** [slander] to the extent of guarding ourselves and others from him. Therefore, the **Poskim** [Halachic Rulings] has written that our being permitted to suspect obtains where harm may befall us or others if we do not suspect him. The aspect of **others** requires extensive explanation. See the **Be'er Mayim Chaim**[73]. But in other instances, aside from fear of harm, it is forbidden to suspect on the basis of **Lashon Hara** [slander] and to believe him - the speaker at all.

---

[72] Niddah 61a
[73] Part Two, Principle 9

Seif 11

And there are many things in which men stumble in the area of **to suspect**, and it merits much discussion, but this is not the place to treat it at length. I shall write about it, Lord willing, below, in the last paragraph. But, in sum, their saying that one must **suspect** in the area of **Lashon Hara** [slander], refers only to guarding oneself against the object of the **Lashon Hara** [slander], but, God forbid, to do anything against him or to cause him harm or shame because of this, great or small, even if the **Lashon Hara** [slander] were spoken of him by a single Kasher witness, who testified about him thus in **Beth-Din** [Court], for one witness is of no avail except for the imposition of an oath and, more than that, even to hate him in his heart because of this - this, too, is forbidden according to the Torah. How much more so can he not exempt himself, because of the **Lashon Hara** [slander], from his obligations to the one spoken of?

Seif 12

And if he already heard **Lashon Hara** [slander] and accepted it in his heart, both in the area of **between man and his Maker** and **between man and his neighbor**, his amendment is that he strengthens himself to remove these things from his heart, that he does not believe them, and to take it upon himself for the future not to accept **Lashon Hara** [slander] anymore about any man of Israel. And he should confess this, and thereby he will correct his transgression of the negative and positive commandments that he was guilty of by accepting **Lashon Hara** [slander], as explained above in the introduction if he has not yet related it to others, see **Be'er Mayim Chayim**.

CHOFETZ — Part One — CHAIM

Principle 7

Opening Comments

In this principle, there will be explained the **Issur** [prohibition] of the acceptance of **Lashon Hara** [slander], whether it was stated before three or before him alone, and the **Din** [the law] if he heard it from many people or it was publicized in the city, or one spoke it **in his innocence**, or the speaker was one who was believed by him as **two witnesses** are. It contains fourteen sections.

Seif 1

The **Issur** [prohibition] of accepting **Lashon Hara** [slander] obtains even if the speaker speaks it in public, before many people. Still, it is not to be concluded because of this that it is true, but the bearers must suspect that it might be true and probe the matter. And if it becomes clear to them that it is true, they should reprove him the object of the **Lashon Hara** [slander] for it - That is, for what he has done or said.

Seif 2

There is no **Heter** [a halachic permit] to believe **Lashon Hara** [slander], even if the speaker spoke it to his face since we have heard no acknowledgment of this from the one spoken about, how much more so are we not to believe it if the speaker is not now before him, but only says that he would have spoken it to his face. And, in our many sins, men greatly stumble in this. And even if he

CHOFETZ Part One CHAIM

remains silent now when the demeaning things are said before him, even so, no proof is to be taken from this that what was said was true. And even if it was always his object's nature never to remain silent when he was told something against him, and this time he does remain silent, this is no proof of his guilt, for perhaps, this time, he overcame his nature and resolved **not to answer to the quarrel**, or perhaps he saw that certainly, they would believe the words of the speaker rather than his - as is the nature of the world, it is commonly held that if one but speak the things to the other's face, even if the other deny them a hundred times, he will be believed no more - Wherefore he took counsel with himself that it was better to remain silent and be of the company of **the shamed**. This being so, it is forbidden to take proof from this his silence that the thing is true.

Seif 3

Just as it is forbidden to accept **Lashon Hara** [slander] if he heard it from one, the **Din** [the law] is the same even if he heard it from two or more. And this applies not only when they - the speakers are rendered **evildoers** by their speaking in which instance they are certainly not to be believed for even according to their words that **Ploni** [so and so] acted improperly, they have transgressed - **You shall not go about talebearing**, which applies even to tales that are true, in which instance they themselves are evildoers, so how, then, can we believe them about this Jew, whose status until now was one of absolute **Kashruth** [kosher]? For he who is suspected of having transgressed the negative commandment against **Lashon Hara** [slander] is also suspected of lying, fabricating, and adding. And what of it if they are two? Even if they were many more, **a band of evildoers is not of the count** of **Kosher Jews** - but even if what they say about him is not something for which they are branded **evildoers** if the truth is with them, even so, it is forbidden to accept their words and to believe them implicitly, for, even if they are two or more, the title **witnesses** can be ascribed only to those who testify in **Beth-Din** [Court], but not to those who testify outside of **Beth-Din** [Court], who, even if they speak falsely, are not called - **false witnesses**, but **spreaders of an evil name** alone. All this, as far as belief is concerned, but to suspect is permitted, even if he heard it from one alone.

Seif 4

The same is true if a rumor has spread about someone that he has done something or said something not in accordance with the Torah, whether a greater or lesser **Issur** [prohibition], it is forbidden to accept it, to believe it implicitly, but only to suspect until the thing is clarified. How much more so must he take care, if he wishes to tell the something to others, that he has no intention to spread the rumor and to reveal it further, as we explained above[74].

Seif 5

All this that we have said applies to a Jew in general, but if he were already known from the past to be an evildoer, it having been revealed about him several times that he transgressed flagrantly **Issurim** [prohibitions] known to all of Israel to be forbidden, such as fornication and the like - about such a man it is permitted to accept **Lashon**

---

[74] Principle 2, section 2

Hara [slander].

Seif 6
And if one comes to him and tells him of his affairs, and includes something demeaning both to himself and to his friend, he is permitted to believe only what applies to himself and not what applies to his friend.

Seif 7
And now we shall begin to explain, with the help of the Lord, the **Din** [the law] of accepting **Lashon Hara** [slander] from a man who is believed like two witnesses, or from someone speaking **in his innocence**, or if there are elements in what is said which indicate it to be true. And though in most of their **Dinim** [the laws] they are alike, I have divided each one into sections by themselves, for there are several details in which each one is different from the other, and also so that the eyes of the reader not be overtaxed by the abundance of branches which spread from each one. And this I have begun with the help of Him who graces man with knowledge. The **Issur** [prohibition] of **Lashon Hara** [slander] obtains even if it is heard from one who is believed to the hearer like two witnesses. As to what we have written above[75], it is permitted to reveal the matter secretly to his Rabbi or to his close confidant if he knows that his words will be believed like those of two witnesses and that it is permitted for his Rabbi to accept his words and to hate him the object of the **Lashon Hara** [slander], and to distance himself from his company, until it becomes known to him that he has repented of his evil way - that

---
[75] Principle 4, section 5

is there, where it is a thing because of which he is, in truth, permitted to speak demeaningly of him if he has not repented, since he knowingly transgressed something which is known by all of Israel to be forbidden, in which instance no merit is to be posited of him as in the act in the Talmud of **Toviyah**[76], which is an act of fornication, and the like. Not so, where it is a thing where some merit is to be posited of him, such as lacking knowledge of the **Issur** [prohibition] of the act, or, perhaps, having performed the act unwittingly. Nor is it permitted to speak of him demeaningly in general, or as lacking in advantages, as mentioned before[77], or to bring up the - Negative acts of his forbears or his relatives, or his early - Negative deeds. Certainly, **being believed like two** does not apply in these instances. For what difference does it make if this That is, what is said about him in these instances is not false at all? In spite of this, the Torah forbade speaking of him demeaningly because of this but legislated to judge him only on the scales of merit in such things, as explained before[78]. And the hearer as well as the speaker is also forbidden to think demeaningly of his friend in his heart because of this[79]. And aside from the **Issur** [prohibition] of accepting the **Lashon Hara** [slander], he transgresses - Before[80] the blind man does not place a stumbling block. along with many other positive and negative commandments, as explained above in the introduction. For the speaker certainly transgresses the **Issur** [prohibition] of **Lashon Hara**

---

[76] Pesachim, 113b
[77] Principle 5, section 2
[78] Principle 5, section 3
[79] Principle 6, section 7
[80] Leviticus 19:14

[slander], as explained by all the **Poskim** [Halachic Rulings], to the effect that **Lashon Hara** [slander] is forbidden even if true, and he the accepter brings him - the speaker to this **Issur** [prohibition]. For if he - refused to listen, his friend - the speaker would not arrive at this **Issur** [prohibition] at all. And the more the words of the speaker are accepted and his - the speaker's act is effectual, to that extent the accepter's act is more severe, for through him his friend is brought to such a great **Issur** [prohibition].

Seif 8

And even if what is spoken of is like the act of **Toviyah**[81], it is not permitted to be accepted categorically, but only with the two following qualifications -

> **A.** only if he - the speaker tells him that he himself saw the thing, but if he heard it from others, this speaker has no advantage at all.
>
> **B.** Even if he told him that he saw it himself, it is permitted only to believe him and to distance himself from his - the sinner's company until it is known that he repented of his evil way, but not to go and reveal it to others[82]. How much more so is it not permitted to cause him monetary loss or to strike him, God forbid, because of this?

Seif 9

And if the one who spoke the **Lashon Hara** [slander] spoke it **in his innocence**. This will be explained in the **Be'er Mayim Chayim**, the **Din** [the law] is as follows -

---

[81] Pesachim, 113b
[82] Principle 4, section 5

If in this matter, even if it be true, there is reason to judge him in the scales of merit, or if it concerns the negation of advantages, or one of the other instances that we explained in section 7 if this speaker did not see the thing itself but only heard it from others, certainly it is forbidden to accept it from him and to believe it in his heart as demeaning to his friend. And even if none of these particulars obtain, still, he must take care not to accept from one **speaking in his innocence** anything demeaning about his friend. And it certainly is forbidden to rely on this to go afterward and tell this to others or to shame him with words because of this. And how much more so is it forbidden to cause him monetary loss or to strike him, God forbid, which is definitely forbidden according to the Torah?

Seif 10

And if there are **indications** that what is said about him is true, the **Din** [the law] is as follows - Even if there is in this matter, even if it be true, a reason to judge him in the scale of merit, or if it concerns the negation of advantages, or one of the other instances that we explained above in section 7, **indications** do not apply here, for certainly we must judge him in the scales of merit, since he is a **mediocre** man and not a confirmed evildoer, so that he not be shamed in our eyes because of this, as mentioned above. But if it is a thing where no element of merit can be found for the doer, it is permitted to believe and to accept.

Seif 11

And this applies only if they are real indications, that is, only if they relate directly to the story, and he saw them himself. But if they are far from it the story and are only slight indications, or if he did not see them himself, but only heard about them from others, he has no advantage in this towards acceptance at all.

Seif 12

And know that even with **real indications**, this is of avail only as far as being permitted to believe himself the thing that is told him, but as far as going afterward and telling it to others, it is of no avail. For it has no advantage over him himself seeing something demeaning in his friend, in which instance he is forbidden afterward to tell others, as explained above[83]. And know further that in any case it is forbidden to rely upon this hater of **real indications** to cause him monetary loss thereby or to strike him.

Seif 13

Sometimes permission is given to **Beth-Din** [Court] to smite one because of **the exigencies of the hour**. As when one comes to cry out before them over something stolen from him, having as he says **real indications** that **Ploni** [so and so] stole the thing from him. And **Beth-Din** [Court], too, see the indications, or witnesses testify to them as to their presence. In such an instance, permission was given to them **Beth-Din** [Court] to administer stripes to the accused so that he confesses. But an individual, and even **Beth-Din** [Court], if the **indications** have not been confirmed by them, but only by the claimant, have not been given this permission.

---

[83] Principle 4 section 4

Seif 14

And from this, you will see how many people err in these things to the extent that if something is stolen from them, and they suspect someone, they tell the city dignitaries that they have **indications** against him, and they **beat and punish** not in accordance with the **Din** [the law] to make him confess. And, in truth, this is not in accordance with the **Din** [the law]. For if **indications** were like proof of the act of theft itself and the city dignitaries are considered like **Beth-Din** [Court], would they not have to know first that the object was stolen? Would witnesses to the **indications** not be required, or do they themselves have to see the **indications**? as in the story in the Talmud of **Mar**[84] **Zutra**, but not rely on the claimant and smite a Jew in vain. And even only to believe the claimant in their heart that this man stole from him is forbidden because of acceptance of **Lashon Hara** [slander]. How much more so, to rely upon this and to beat him, whereby they perform a great **Issur** [prohibition] and transgress the negative commandment of - He[85] shall not smite more.

---

[84] Sanhedrin 46a
[85] Devarim 25:3

CHOFETZ Part One CHAIM

Principle 8

Opening Comments

In this principle, there will be explained the **Issur** [prohibition] of speaking **Lashon Hara** [slander], in all of its aspects. It contains fourteen sections. In the foregoing principle, we have explained what is called - **Lashon Hara** [slander], in all of its aspects, and, likewise, the **Din** [the law] against accepting **Lashon Hara** [slander]. And now, in this principle, we shall explain the **Issur** [prohibition] of speaking **Lashon Hara** [slander], which the Torah forbade us - The nature of the speaker, the one spoken of, and the one before whom it is spoken, all in order. And, likewise, we shall explain the acceptance of **Lashon Hara** [slander]. Therefore, let it not be cause for wonder in the eyes of the reader that I sometimes write something very simple. This is so that the sequence of things is consistent or because it is something that many err in. Also, if he reads carefully, he will find at the end of each subject something new. First, we shall explain the nature of the speaker.

Seif 1
There is no difference, in the **Issur** [prohibition] of speaking **Lashon Hara** [slander], as to whether the speaker is a man or a woman, a relative or not related, though commonly one who is demeaned will not take offense if the speaker is motivated by the family love that unites them. And it is also the way of a relative that when he speaks to one about his kin, his intent is not to demean

him, but to be zealous for the truth, it being his view that his relative acted wrongly to another in a certain matter. Still, if he - the speaker erred in judgment in this respect, that is, if he was too hasty to incriminate his relative when he was really guiltless, this does not leave the category of absolute **Lashon Hara** [slander].

Seif 2

And now we shall begin to explain against whom the Torah forbids speaking **Lashon Hara** [slander]. The **Issur** [prohibition] of **Lashon Hara** [slander] applies both to speaking against a man and speaking against a woman. And there is no difference in this between his own wife or someone else's wife. And many go astray in this, in our many sins, it is permitted in their eyes to speak demeaningly of his wife and his father in laws house before his brothers and his father's house. But according to the **Din** [the law] there is no difference in this if not that he intends in this, future benefit, and not to demean them, and also that there be no admixture of falsehood in his words. And his entire **Din** [the law] is according to what is explained below[86].

Seif 3

And sometimes the **Issur** [prohibition] of speaking **Lashon Hara** [slander] applies even if spoken against a minor - As to speak demeaningly of a small orphan whom others are raising in their house. For this **Lashon Hara** [slander] may lead to their driving him out. And all such instances, where through his speaking the minor may be harmed or aggrieved. And as to the **Din** [the law] if what

---

[86] Principle 10, section 6

he says of the minor is public knowledge, see above[87]. And if he intends by his speaking to prevent damage that this minor is prone to cause and to guide him in a just path, he is permitted to speak thus. But he must know clearly in the beginning that what he says is true and not rely on what he has heard from others, as will be explained below[88]. He must also be able to project what his words will lead to, for very often **a crooked judgment** results from these things.

Seif 4

And know that the **Issur** [prohibition] of speaking **Lashon Hara** [slander] applies even against an **Am Haaretz** [ignoramus]. For he, too, is in the category of **the people of the Lord and His hosts** that He took out of Egypt. How much more so, if someone speaks **Lashon Hara** [slander] against a Torah scholar is his sin extremely severe? And **Chazal** [Sages] have said in the Talmud - All[89] who speak **Lashon Hara** [slander] after the burial litter of a Torah scholar fall into Gehinnom. And many times, he comes through this to shame a Torah scholar. And the greatness of the punishment of shaming a Torah scholar is well known in the Talmud - To[90] the effect that shaming a Torah scholar is in the category of - For[91] the word of the Lord has he shamed... Cut off shall be that soul. But the evil inclination entices men into believing that the **Din** [the law] of shaming a Torah scholar applies only in the time of the Talmud when they

---

[87] Principle 2, section 3 and section 9, and Part 2, Principle 2, section 3
[88] Principle 10
[89] Berachoth 19a
[90] Sanhedrin 99b
[91] Bamidbar 15:31

were exceptionally wise, but not to those in our times. And this is a great error, for every - **Torah scholar** is called thus relative to the generation. And even in our generation, if he is only fit to teach and toils in Torah, he is called a Torah scholar. And if one shames him, even with words in general, even not to his face, he has committed a grave sin and is liable in **Shulchan Aruch** to Ex-communication - How[92] much more so if this Torah scholar is the **Posek** [Halachic Rulings] of the city, in which case the **Issur** [prohibition] of one who shames him is even greater. For aside from the fact that he must regard him as a sage and accord him honor since he relies upon his rulings when he speaks demeaningly of him, he keeps the public from the service of the Lord. For through this **Lashon Hara** [slander], the rest of the people will say - Why should we go and ask him to rule upon the Torah disputes between us, when he cannot even mediate between us? And because of this everyone will build a **sacrificial mound** for himself. Along with other corruptions, too numerous to mention, the Lord protects us.

Seif 5

And this entire **Issur** [prohibition] of **Lashon Hara** [slander] applies only when spoken against the man who is in the category of **Amitecha** [your neighbor], **Shetecha** [with you], a people who are with you in Torah and in Mitzvoth. But those people whom he knows to have **Apikorsoth** [heresy] among them, it is a Mitzvah to demean and to shame, both in their presence and not in their presence, in everything that he sees or hears about

---

[92] Yoreh Deah 243:7

them. For it is written - And[93] you shall not wrong one man his **Amito** [fellow]. And - You[94] shall not go talebearing among **B'eamecha** [your people]. And they are not in this category, for they do not act as Your people. And it is written - Do[95] I not hate your haters - O Lord - And against those who rise up against You do I strive. And one who denies the Torah and prophecy of Israel, both the written and the oral Law, is called an **Apikoress** [heretic], even if he says all the Torah is from Heaven, except for one verse, or one **Kal Vachomer** [a fortiori argument], or one **Gezeirah Shavah** [identity deduction], or one **Dikduk** [inference].

Seif 6

And the above applies only if he himself heard from them words of heresy, but if others told him, it is forbidden to rely upon this to demean them, both in their presence or not in their presence. And he is also not to believe this in his heart, as in the **Din** [the law] of acceptance of **Lashon**[96] **Hara** [slander]. But he must take care in the interim to suspect them and also to warn others in secret not to join them in the interim until thing is clarified. And all this applies to hearing in general, but if they have acknowledged heretics in the city, his **Din** [the law] is as if he knew - and heard the heresy from them himself.

Seif 7

And know also that if one is acknowledged in the city to be an evildoer, because of other transgressions which it is

---

[93] Vayikra 25:17
[94] Vayikra 19:16
[95] Tehillim 139:21
[96] Principle 5

CHOFETZ — Part One — CHAIM

permitted to demean him for, the **Din** [the law] is the same. And who is **acknowledged**? One whom the people of the city agree to be an evildoer beyond doubt - because of evil reports that are always spread about him in the area of fornication and the like, things which all of Israel know to be forbidden. But if a rumor, in general, were heard about him, it is forbidden to rely upon this to demean him, God forbid, and even to believe it in one's heart is forbidden, as we have explained above[97]. And even though I greatly feared to write this **Heter** [a halachic permit] down because of **the men of the tongue**, who, as soon as they hear about anyone a trace of something wrong, immediately brand the man as **acknowledged** in wickedness, and they will demean him and attribute the **Heter** [a halachic permit] to this book; notwithstanding this, I have not omitted it, in accordance with what **Chazal** [Sages] said in the Talmud about Rabban Yochanan ben Zakkai - He[98] said it something **risky**, analogous to the above, and in accordance with this verse did he say it - For[99] the ways of the Lord are just. The righteous shall walk in them, and the offenders **the men of the tongue** in our instance, shall stumble in them.

Seif 8

And know, that others saying that it is permitted to speak **Lashon Hara** [slander] against - **men of contention** applies only if by revealing to men the contender's great deception in this matter and they see that the **Din** [the law] is not with them, the contention will cease. But,

---

[97] Principle 7
[98] Bava Bathra 89b
[99] Hosea 14:10

failing this, there is no difference in the matter. The following details are also needed for a **Heter** [a halachic permit -

> **A.** that the things which convince him that they are **men of contention** be known by himself and not by reliance upon what he hears from others unless it is clear to him that what they say is true.
> **B.** He must intend the aforementioned benefit and not be motivated by hatred.
> **C.** If it is possible for him to silence the quarrel in a different way, without having to speak against them, such as reproof and the like, he is forbidden to speak **Lashon Hara** [slander] against them - unless he is afraid to reprove them, lest, when **the men of contention** see that he is not in agreement with them, they will annul his counsel until he is left with no further recourse to settle the matter. But in such an instance, he must exercise great discretion and not hastily decide to call one party to the dispute **men of contention**. But he must judge carefully, according to the Torah, who are the **men of contention**. And if he cannot decide who is right. **Sit and do nothing** is the preferred course.

Seif 9

And know further, that even to shame and insult the dead is forbidden. And the **Poskim** [Halachic Rulings] has written that there is a prohibition and a ban on the early masters not to defame or spread an evil report about the dead. All this, even if the dead one was an ignoramus; how much more so, if he were a Torah scholar, is the one who shames him guilty of a great sin and liable to the ban for this? As stated in **Shulchan Aruch** - And[100] the **Issur** [prohibition] of shaming a Torah scholar obtains even if he shames the scholar himself, how much more so is it forbidden to shame his words of Torah.

Seif 10

And now we shall explain before whom it is forbidden to speak **Lashon Hara** [slander]. There is no difference in the **Issur** [prohibition] of telling, whether he speaks it to others, relatives or non-relatives, or to his wife unless there be some future benefit to be derived from it. For example, if she gives credit to bad people, whom it will be difficult to collect from later, for which reason he tells her of their bad nature and warns her not to give them credit. The same applies to one partner telling the other about certain people that in his opinion they are not trustworthy, and the like in the Talmud - Do[101] not allow the students of Rabbi Meir to come in here, because they are contentious, etc. And even if he himself does not recognize their bad nature but has only heard of them, he is also permitted to tell her and to warn her for the future, even though he is not permitted to believe implicitly what he has heard about them, but in any event, he must suspect. But in this instance, he must not tell her in such a way that implies that he believes implicitly what he has heard, but he should only say to her - I have heard this and this about that man, therefore, be careful not to give him credit. But without this, there is no difference in this matter between his wife and others. But many err in this,

---

[100] Yoreh Deah 243:7
[101] Kiddushin 52b

telling their wives everything that has happened to them with this man and that in the house of study or in the marketplace. Now, aside from the **Issur** [prohibition] of **Lashon Hara** [slander], he also stirs up contention thereby. For she will certainly harbor hatred and quarrel because of this with that man or with the members of his household. And she will also incite him to go again and quarrel with that man because of this. And, in the end, she herself will shame him thereby. Therefore, one who is circumspect will guard himself greatly, not to reveal such matters to his wife.

Seif 11

And there is no difference in this **Issur** [prohibition] as to whether he tells people who are not relatives of the man spoken of or his relatives. And even for one to speak about his brother before his father is **Lashon Hara** [slander]. Even if he intends by his say that his relatives reprove him for this, it is also forbidden. For he should have reproved him first by himself and not immediately gone to speak his shame - unless he assumed that his reproof would be of no avail, in which case it is permitted.

Seif 12

And know also that the **Issur** [prohibition] of **Lashon Hara** [slander] obtains even if he demeans him before a Jew, how much more so if he demeans him before gentiles. Aside from his shaming the honor of Israel and desecrating the honor of Heaven thereby, he also causes great evil thereby to his friend. For if he speaks demeaningly of his friend before a Jew, he will not be immediately believed. But if he speaks about a Jew to a gentile, telling him that this Jew is a deceiver and a wronger of men and the like, he will believe this immediately and spread it to all and cause him harm and grief. How much more so, if he goes and informs against a Jew before gentiles, is his sin too great to bear? For he enters by this into the class of **the informers**, and his **Din** [the law] is like that of a heretic and of those who deny Torah and the resurrection, as it says in Talmud - Gehinnom[102] ending but they not ending. Therefore, every many of Israel must greatly guard himself against this. And one who transgresses this and goes and informs against a Jew before them is like one who would insult and blaspheme and lift his hand against Moshe Rabbeinu, may peace be upon him **Shulchan**[103] **Aruch**.

Seif 13

And now we shall explain the **Din** [the law] of accepting **Lashon Hara** [slander]. The acceptance of **Lashon Hara** [slander], which the Torah exhorted us against, is not to believe in one's heart that the thing said is true. There is no need to expatiate upon the difference between the nature of the accepter and that of the man whom he accepts about. For there is almost no difference. But, the principle of the thing, in short, is this. Every Jew is commanded not to accept **Lashon Hara** [slander] against any other Jew - except about heretics, informers, and the like - those who have left the category of **your fellow**.

Seif 14

There is also no difference in the acceptance of **Lashon**

---

[102] Rosh Hashana 17a
[103] Choshen Mishpat 26

Hara [slander] as to whether he heard it from others or from his father, his mother, or the members of his household. More than this, we find in the Midrash - That[104] if a man saw his father and mother speaking **superfluous words**, such as **Lashon Hara** [slander] and the like, aside from being exhorted not to accept their words, he is exhorted to prevent them from speaking these words. And if he remains silent, both he and they are greatly punished. And it is stated in the Talmud - That[105] one who should protest against the men of his household but does not is caught for punishment in time to come for the men of his household. That is why a man should always be accustomed in his house to reprove for these things, but only gently, and to present before them the greatness of the punishment for this in time to come, and the greatness of the reward for one who keeps himself from this. And he should, especially, always take heed of himself, that the members of his household never hear from his mouth anything demeaning against his friend. For if he himself transgresses this, aside from the **Issur** [prohibition] itself, he himself becomes a great obstruction. For he will never again have a justification for reproving them for this. And, for the most part, the conduct of the members of the household in such things is patterned after the conduct of the head of the household himself. Therefore, he himself must take great care in this, and it shall go well for him in this world, and the next.

---

[104] Tanna D'bei Eliyahu 28
[105] Shabbath 54b

CHOFETZ   Part One   CHAIM

Principle 9

Opening Comments

In this principle there will be explained **Avak** [dust] **Lashon Hara** [slander]. the **Avak** [dust] **of Lashon Hara** [slander], in all of its details. It contains six sections.

Seif 1
There are things that are forbidden because of the **Avak** [dust] of **Lashon Hara** [slander]. As when one says about another - Who would have said about **Ploni** [so and so] that he would be the way he is now? or - Don't talk about **Ploni** [so and so]. I do not want to talk about what happened or what will happen, and the like. Also, in the category of the **Avak** [dust] of **Lashon Hara** [slander] is speaking in one's praise before his enemies, for this will cause them to speak demeaningly of him. And it is forbidden to be profuse in praise of him, even if not before his enemies, for through this he will come to demean him in the end, saying - Except for this one bad trait that he has. Or the listeners will say - Why do you speak so much in his praise? Does he not have this and this trait?

Seif 2
All this, if he does not praise him in public. But in public, it is forbidden in all cases. For in a gathering of many people, there are bound to be found both **rightists** and **leftists**, or enviers, and by speaking in his praise, they the latter will come to speak demeaningly of him. And if he

wishes to praise a man who is acknowledged by all and known to be kosher and a Tzaddik, in whom no evil or fault is to be found, then even before an enemy and an envier he is to be praised, for he will not be able to demean him. And if he does demean him, all will know that he has spoken falsely.

Seif 3

One must also take care not to praise his friend with praise that leads to loss, as in a guest's going out to the city square and proclaiming to all how lavishly his host entertained him with food and drink and how many pains, he took for him. For through this, **empty** men will gather and converge upon the host and consume his fare. Of one such as this it is written - He[106] who blesses his friend in a loud voice early in the morning, it will be accounted a curse to him. And from this it may be derived that the same is true of one who received a loan from his friend and publicized to all his great generosity. For through this many disreputable men will converge upon him and he will not be able to put them off. And one must heed his mouth and his tongue not to be suspect in his words and not to be regarded as a speaker of **Lashon Hara** [slander]. And if he brings himself to be suspected, this is in the category of the **Avak** [dust] of **Lashon Hara** [slander].

Seif 4

It is forbidden to live in a neighborhood of men of **Lashon Hara** [slander], how much more so to sit with them and hear their words, since he inclines his ears to hear, even if he does not intend to accept what they say

---

[106] Mishlei 27:14

above[107]. And if he knows about one of his students that he is one of **the men of the tongue**, he must distance him from himself if he knows that reproof will not avail him. And if by some mischance he was **caught** in a company of **men of the tongue** and heard them speaking **Lashon Hara** [slander] - if he assumes that his reproof may avail to stop them, he certainly must reprove them according to the **Din** [the law] of the Torah. And even if he assumes that his reproof will not avail to stop them, but that he will not make matters worse by reproving them, here, too, he may not remain silent, lest they assume that he is like they are and acquiesces in what they say. How much more must he answer and rebuke them in defense of the honor of an innocent man and a Tzaddik, whom they criticize? This is one of the reasons that one must leave the company of evildoers - for he will be punished for hearing their words and failing to criticize them.

Seif 5
And know that even if he heard his young son and daughter speaking **Lashon Hara** [slander], it is a Mitzvah to rebuke them and to stop them, as it is written - Guide[108] the youth according to his bent. As it is explained in **Shulchan**[109] **Aruch** in connection with all the **Issurim** [prohibitions] in the Torah.

Seif 6
If one tells his friend anything, he is forbidden to repeat

---

[107] Principle 6, section 2
[108] Mishlei 22:6
[109] Orach Chaim 343:1

it to others, unless he gave him permission to do so. And this, only if it contains no **Lashon Hara** [slander].

CHOFETZ   Part One   CHAIM

Principle 10

Opening Comments

In this principle there will be explained some of the details of **Avak** [dust] **Lashon Hara** [slander] between man and his neighbor - that is, if one stole from his neighbor or wronged him or the like, or if someone stole from him or wronged him or insulted him - how is it permitted to reveal this to others.

Above[110], we explained the **Din** [the law] of **Lashon Hara** [slander] in the area of **between man and his Maker**. Now we shall begin, with the Lord's help, to explain the **Din** [the law] in the area of **between man and his neighbor**. We have divided this into a principle by itself because its **Din** [the law] is different in many ways. This I begin with the help of Him who grants a man knowledge.

Seif 1

If a man saw someone harming his friend, whether robbing him, wronging him, or causing him damage, whether the one robbed or caused damage knew of it or not - or if he shamed him or aggrieved him, or wronged him with words - and it became known to him clearly that he did not return the theft or reimburse him for the damage and did not beseech him to forgive his transgression - even if he saw this thing by himself, he can relate it to others in order to help the one who was wronged and to condemn these evil deeds before men, but

---

[110] Principle 5

CHOFETZ — Part One — CHAIM

he must take care that there not be lacking the following seven details which we shall now explain:

Seif 2

A. that he sees the thing himself and does not hear of it from others unless it becomes clear to him afterward that the thing is true.

B. that he takes great care not to immediately determine the thing to be theft, or wronging, or damage, and the like, without carefully analyzing whether it actually is theft or damage according to the **Din** [the law].

C. that he reproves the sinner first, gently - perhaps it the proof will avail him and he will thereby rectify his ways. And if he does not listen to him, then he should apprise the people of this man's guilt - how he deliberately harmed his friend. And if he knows that his reproof will not be accepted - this will be explained below[111].

D. that he should not exaggerate the wrong beyond what it is.

E. that he should intend the benefit of others and not, God forbid, to benefit himself from the taint he ascribes to his friend, and not out of hatred that he bears him from before.

F. if he can bring about the desired benefit itself without recourse to exposing him for his act, then, in all instances, it is forbidden to speak of what he did.

G. that he should not cause the one spoken about more damage than he would suffer if the matter

---

[111] section 7

were brought to trial in **Beth-Din** [Court]. The rationale for this is to be found below[112] in the laws of **Rechiluth** [Gossip], where it properly belongs.

Seif 3

And all this applies only if the one who saw him were better than he. But if he were a sinner such as he, and also **sick** in such transgressions as he, it is forbidden for him to expose him. For the intent of a man like this in revealing his hidden things is not for the sake of good and fear of God, but to rejoice in the other's misfortune and to shame him for it. About such things it has already been said - And[113] I shall visit the blood of **Y'izreel** upon the house of **Yehu**. For even though **Yehu** performed a Mitzvah by cutting off the house of **Achav** in **Y'izreel**, having been commanded to do so by a prophet for which he was awarded the kingdom for four generations, as it is written - Because[114] you have done to the house of **Achav** as was in My heart, children of the fourth generation after you shall sit upon the throne of Israel. Still, the blood of **Achav** was visited upon him in the end, for he, too, was a great offender.

Seif 4

The fifth detail that we wrote of above, namely, that he intends to benefit, is as we shall explain. That is, if the people to whom he tells the story can help the one who was robbed, wronged, damaged, or shamed, then certainly it is correct to do this - That is, to expose the

---

[112] Principle 9
[113] Hoshea 1:4
[114] Kings-B 10:30

perpetrator. And even if this benefit cannot result through his telling, his intent is that people distance themselves from the way of wickedness when they hear of it for people condemn doers of wrong, and perhaps he himself will repent through this of his evil ways and correct his deeds when he hears others condemning him the offender for this - If this is his motivation, then this, too, is not in the category of **Lashon Hara** [slander] and is considered a benefit, since, in any event, his intent is not to derive pleasure from this taint that he ascribes to his friend, but only to be zealous for the truth, that perhaps some future benefit will result. But if he assumes that of a certainty no benefit will result - as when the people he tells it to are also men of wickedness, that they, too, have many times done such evil to people, and they do not consider it a sin at all - to such people, he must be careful not to speak of this matter at all. Aside from the fact that no benefit will result from his doing so, great damage may yet result from this. For they may go and relate it to the thief or the wringer or the shamer and they will thereby transgress **You shall not go talebearing among your people**. And also, through this, great quarrels are likely to result. And, especially, if, God forbid, this can lead to informing, even if all the above details are satisfied, it is forbidden to say anything. And know that there is no difference in all of these details as to whether he is asked by the robbed or the damaged or the shamed to **investigate** the cause of his damage or his shame, or if he is not asked. For where to tell is permitted, it is permitted even if he were not asked. And where it is forbidden that is, where all of the above details were not satisfied, it is not permitted even if he were asked. And even if he is his relative, it is still forbidden. Many people go astray in this. For if they hear that someone did something to their relative, then even if it is not clear to them what the truth is or what the cause is, they immediately go and requite the offender with evil, thinking that they thereby fulfill the Mitzvah of - And[115] from your flesh, you shall not conceal yourself. They thereby fall into great error, for there is no difference between relative and non-relative in all of the above **Dinim** [the laws]. For - And from your flesh, you shall not conceal yourself was not said in order to commit an **Issur** [prohibition], God forbid.

Seif 5

And also, if he sees one speaking **Lashon Hara** [slander] against his friend, this, too - That is, speaking **Lashon Hara** [slander], is one of the transgressions between **man and his neighbor**. Therefore, if all the above details have been satisfied, it is permitted to publicize the great wrong of the speaker. And all this does not avail to permit it unless the thing has already come to the ears of the one spoken of. But if not, he may not relate it even to others, for **your friend has a friend**, etc., and it is bound to be revealed to him, too, and is in the category of **Rechiluth** [Gossip]. How much more so is it forbidden to reveal it to the man spoken of himself, even if his motivation **Be Zeal** [begrudge] for the truth? For this is absolute **Rechiluth** [Gossip], even if one of the low-lives mocks one of the most eminent men in Israel, even if he be his father or his teacher.

Seif 6

And sometimes it is permitted to tell the thing to others

---

[115] Isaiah 58:7

even if it has not yet come to the ears of the one spoken about. As when he sees that absolute benefit will accrue to him -the latter, and, also, that the aforementioned details are not lacking[116]. And I shall explain what I mean by **benefit**, so that the reader not come to err in this. As when he knows the nature of the talebearer and the nature of the story, that just as he demeans him to his face, so will he go afterward and demean him further before others, especially in that we mentioned that he must first reprove him, and he did so, and his words were not accepted. And it is well known, in our many sins, that almost all of us stumble into **Lashon Hara** [slander], especially the acceptance of **Lashon Hara** [slander] so that it is likely that his **Lashon Hara** [slander] will be accepted, and it will be very difficult afterward to remove it from their ears, for - **the first in the quarrel is right**. Therefore, it is certainly fitting that he comes first to those people and set forth before them the great wrong of the talebearer and relate before them how he demeans that innocent man, so that when the talebearer afterward comes to them and tells them his story, they will not accept his words, and, to the contrary, will reprove him to his face. And, certainly, when he sees that his words are not being accepted and are also causing him shame and disgrace, he will guard himself against this in the future. This is certainly permitted, for he will thereby rescue the one spoken about from grief and shame, and also the souls of the speaker and the accepter from the **Din** [the law] of Gehinnom, and they the later hearers will also fulfill in him - the speaker the positive commandment of reproof.

---

[116] see Be'er Mayim Chayim

CHOFETZ — Part One — CHAIM

Seif 7

And now we shall explain the third detail that we mentioned above[117], that he must reprove him first. This applies in general, but if he knows him to be one who will not be chastened by his words and will not accept his reproof, he need not reprove him. But he must take care to relate this thing That is, what he saw in the presence of three. The rationale: If he relates it in the presence of one or two, it would seem as if his intent were that his relating it to them not reach the ears of the accused and that he wanted to flatter him or to deceive him, wherefore he demeans him in secret; and it seems as if he enjoys speaking **Lashon Hara** [slander] against his friend. Another reason - They will come to suspect him and say that the thing - That is, his accusation is certainly not true and that he is inventing the whole thing. For, otherwise, why did he not say it to his face first? And if so, his telling them would not achieve any of the benefits described above[118]. Therefore, the thing must be said in public, that is, before three. For this is as if he were to say it to his face, and he will no longer be suspected. For it is rare to find a man who is Kasher, saying something completely false in public. And though, even now, the hearers are forbidden to believe what he says implicitly so that the accused is demeaned in their heart, as explained above[119], for it may be that even though the story is not completely false, it may be lacking a single detail which may change the picture from beginning to end wherefore they are forbidden to believe the story implicitly, to his discredit,

---

[117] Seif 2
[118] Section 4
[119] Principle 7, section 1

still, it the story should enter their ears for this purpose: that they undertake to investigate whether it is true and reprove that man of whom such evil things are spoken. Perhaps he will heed their words along with other **benefits** mentioned above[120].

Seif 8
And all this, when he is not in fear of the man he talks about, but if he is in fear of him, it being in his power to hurt him, it is possible that leniency may be exercised to permit him to relate the wrong that he the accused did to his friend, even not before three.

Seif 9
And if the teller is known by all to fear no man, and that everything that he would say not in the presence of his friend he would say to his face and fear no one, and he is also held among his people to be a man who speaks only the truth, it is permitted for him to tell men of the wrong he the accused did to his friend, even not in the presence of three. For the hearers will not suspect a man like this of being a flatterer or a liar, but that his intent is only to be zealous for the truth and to help the one who was wronged and to condemn the evil deeds before all. But in this and in all that we wrote in section 8, great care must be taken that there not be lacking any of the details that we mentioned at the beginning of the section, for we have omitted from them only the detail of **before three**.

Seif 10
And know further that the **Din** [the law] of speaking

---
[120] Section 4

Lashon Hara [slander] in the instance of a sin **between man and his neighbor** and in that of a sin **between man and his Maker** is the same, except that in a sin between man and his Maker, it is not permitted to speak **Lashon Hara** [slander] against him even if all the aforementioned details in section 2 were satisfied, unless he saw him holding on to that sin and doing it several times wittingly, and it was known to all that it was an **Issur** [prohibition] see above[121], where we explained this in all of its details.

Seif 11

And how much must one take care not to permit himself to tell others that he had some business with this and this man, and he robbed him or wronged him in this and this way, or that he insulted him or aggrieved him or shamed him and the like. And he is forbidden to relate this even if he knows in himself that he is not falsifying in what he says, and it is forbidden even if there are superadded to this all the other details of the aforementioned **Heter** [a halachic permit]. For certainly his intent at the time of telling was not for **benefit** - that is, to publicize his friend's taint so that wrongdoers be shamed in the eyes of men so that they take heed not to emulate their evil ways, or so that he himself sees men spurning him so that he thereby repents of his - own evil ways. But his intent is only to shame him in the eyes of men, to make him an object of scorn and shame before them for having **touched** his money or his honor. And the more he sees that his words are accepted by the hearers and that he is thereby made an object of aversion and shame in their eyes, the more he rejoices and finds pleasure in this.

---

[121] Principle 4, section 7

Seif 12

How much more so is he forbidden to relate it if he did nothing actively wrong to him, but did not bestow upon him benefactions which in his eyes he should have bestowed upon him in the form of loans or charity or hospitality and the like. If he goes and relates this to others afterward to demean this man thereby, this is absolute **Lashon Hara** [slander] according to the **Din** [the law], as we wrote above[122], and he also transgresses in this several other negative commandments aside from the **Issur** [prohibition] of **Lashon Hara** [slander], as we explained in the aforementioned principle. And, in our many sins, many go astray in this, as we see in practice - that if one is not accepted as graciously as he would like in one city, then, when he travels later to a different city, he publicizes demeaningly the prominent men of the first city because they did not assist him in his affairs. How much more so, if he defames the whole city in general because of this, is his sin egregious. For the **Issur** [prohibition] of **Lashon Hara** [slander], even if true, as we wrote above, obtains even if he speaks against one man, how much more so if he speaks against an entire city in Israel which is staunch in belief in the Lord, is this sin a grave one.

Seif 13

But in spite of this, it seems to me that if he assumes that by telling others how **Ploni** [so and so] wronged him in money matters or the like, future benefit may result, as when he tells people whose words would be heeded by him - the accused if they reproved him, and through this

---

[122] Principle 5, section 1

he would perhaps return the theft to him or repair the damage and the like - If he assumes this, he is permitted to tell them and to request their assistance in this. And sometimes future benefits may arise even when the consideration is not money, but pain, shame, verbal wronging, and the like. As when it becomes known to him clearly that **Ploni** [so and so] is planning to vilify him for a certain thing. If he tells this to prominent men or to the relatives of **Ploni** [so and so], and explains to them the truth of the matter, so that they themselves can see that the **Din** [the law] is with him, perhaps they will stop him from this. Or even if it is something that has already passed, **Ploni** [so and so] already having vilified him, but he assumes that if he does not speak of it to his relatives or to prominent men, to stop him, he will come to vilify him again - In all such cases and the like, he is permitted to tell this to others, even though by his doing so, his friend will be shamed before the listeners. For this to shame him is not the intent of the speaker, but only to guard himself against monetary loss, pain, or shame.

Seif 14

But how careful must one be that all of the aforementioned conditions not be lacking? For if he is not especially careful, he can easily fall into the snare of the evil inclination and become one of the men of **Lashon Hara** [slander] according to the Torah by means of this **Heter** [a halachic permit]. And because of this, I shall review here explicitly all of the aforementioned conditions, a little expanded. In sum - After he knows that his friend has not yet repented of this thing and that his - own intent is **benefit**, as we have explained, it is permitted to tell - but only if the following conditions are not lacking -

Condition A - that he sees the thing himself and not just hears of it from others. For although he may, in truth, have suffered damage, who knows if he the accused is the one who caused it?

Condition B - to take care not to conclude immediately that what happened is in the category of theft, damage, verbal wronging, shame, or the like; but to search out well from the beginning, by the ways of the Torah if the **Din** [the law] is with him, and that the accused is, indeed, the robber, or the damager, or the shamer, or the like. And perhaps this detail is more difficult to picture than all the rest. For - **a man does not see liability in himself**, and - **All the ways of a man are just in his eyes**. And if he goes astray in this, he finds himself in the category of **Motzi Shem Ra** [one who spreads an evil report] the spreader of a false report, which is graver than the **Issur** [prohibition] of **Lashon Hara** [slander].

Condition C - If he assumes that contesting it with the accused himself might be of benefit, he must speak to him before he makes the matter public.

Condition D – He must take special care, in any event, that the whole story be true, without any admixture of falsehood, and that he not exaggerates the wrong beyond what it is - that is, he must not omit from the story any small detail that he understands to be in favor of his friend. Even though this may not avail to justify his friend - if, in any event, by the hearers knowing of this detail in his favor, he would not be so greatly demeaned before them, and by their not knowing of it, he would be greatly demeaned before them, it would be a great **Issur** [prohibition] to omit this detail. In sum: he must not exaggerate the wrong beyond what it is, and if he does, he is in the category of a speaker of **Lashon Hara** [slander] and transgresses several of the **Issurim** [prohibitions] mentioned in the introductions.

Condition E - He must intend **benefit**. This is the principle upon which all of this **Heter** [a halachic permit] revolves[123].

Condition F - If he can realize this benefit in a different way, whereby he is not compelled to speak about him, then, in any instance, it is forbidden to tell the story. But even if he is compelled to tell the story, he can diminish the wrong so that he the accused not be so greatly demeaned before the hearers, and the hoped-for benefit that results from his story, not be lessened because of this, it is a Mitzvah for him to diminish it and not reveal his entire shame before the hearers, since, even without this, he will derive the hoped-for benefit.

Condition H - He should not cause him more damage through his story than he would suffer if they That is, witnesses testified against him in this manner in **Beth-Din** [Court].

Seif 15

And now, see my brother, how much great judgment he

---

[123] see section 13

requires to determine in what manner to tell the story. For while he is speaking, he stands in great danger of transgressing the **Issur** [prohibition] of speaking **Lashon Hara** [slander] if he does not guard himself to satisfy all the conditions, especially 2 and 4. And it is apparent that about this we can say - Death[124] and life are in the hand of the tongue. And if he does not take counsel with himself before he starts speaking, how to express this, he certainly will fail, God forbid. For at the time - of speaking the power of anger intensifies itself in a man, and it is impossible to prevent this. Therefore, he must be extremely careful to take counsel with himself before speaking, how to utter what he has to say, not to aggrandize the wrong beyond what it is, and to intend **benefit** alone, as we have written in section thirteen.

Seif 16

And from all that we have written, we can see the greatness of the error that people always become involved in - If we see someone speaking **Lashon Hara** [slander] against his friend, not in his presence, and demeaning him - if you ask him - Why are you speaking **Lashon Hara** [slander]? he will immediately reply - Because he, too, spoke against me before this and this man. This is a great error for two reasons. First, the one who told you this may not be believed according to the Torah by reason of acceptance of **Rechiluth** [Gossip], as we have written many times - then how is it permitted for you to go and speak about him because of this? And second, even if the thing were true, that he did speak about you, it is still forbidden to speak **Lashon Hara**

---

[124] Mishlei 18:21

[slander] against him because of this, as we wrote above[125].

Seif 17

If something wrong were done and Reuven came and asked Shimon -Who did this thing? even if he understands that Reuven suspects him of this, he is forbidden to reveal who did it, even if he saw it himself. But he should answer - **I did not do the thing** unless it be a thing which, even if he were not asked and he was not suspected at all, he would nonetheless have to tell him, as in an incident between a man and his neighbor, where all of the seven conditions were met, or one between man and his Maker, where there were satisfied the conditions that we wrote of above[126]. And all of this that we have written is according to the **Din** [the law], but it befits every man of spirit to do what is beyond the letter of the law, and not to remove himself from involvement when there is a possibility that it will become known to the asker who did do the thing, and he - the doer will be shamed because of this. And more than this, we find in Talmud - That[127] several **Tannaim** [Conditions] took the blame upon themselves so that it not be known who the actual sinner was. And so, we find in **Sefer Chassidim** - And[128] if he finds himself in the company of men, and something wrong was done, and it is not known who the sinner is, he should say - **I am the sinner**, even if he did not sin.

---

[125] section 11
[126] Principle 4, sections 5, 7, 8
[127] Sanhedrin 11a
[128] Sefer Chassidim 22

Part Two

The Prohibition Against **Rechiluth** [Gossip]

Principle 1

Opening Comments

In this principle, there will be explained the **Issur** [prohibition] of speaking **Rechiluth** [Gossip], even if it be absolutely true, what is called - **Rechiluth** [Gossip], what to answer if one asks - What did **Ploni** [so and so] say about me? and all the other details of the **Issur** [prohibition].

Seif 1

One who bears tales about his friend transgresses the negative commandment of - Do[1] not deal basely with members of your people. Do not profit by the blood of your fellow. It is a great sin and leads to the killing of many souls in Israel, for which reason it is followed by - You shall not stand by the blood of your neighbor. Go[2] and see what resulted from the **Rechiluth**[3] [Gossip] of **Doeg the Edomite**, because of which there was wiped out the entire city of Nov was, the city of Cohanim. And this negative commandment which we have adduced is that which the Torah wrote explicitly for this **Issur**

---

[1] Vayikra 19:16
[2] Rambam, Hilchoth Deoth 8
[3] I Samuel-A 21

[prohibition]. But aside from this, there are many other relevant negative and positive commandments, as explained above in the introduction.

Seif 2

What is **Rachil** [talebearing]? Peddling things from one to another and saying - This and this is what **Ploni** [so and so said about you. This is what **Ploni** [so and so] did to you. This and this are what I heard that he did to you or wants to do to you. Even though this may not be demeaning to the one spoken about, even according to the words of the talebearer, and even if he himself - the one spoken about were asked, he would not deny it - either because the truth and the right are with him - or because he intended something else than what is assumed by these acts or words - still, he is called a **Rachil** [talebearing].

Seif 3

And know that the **Issur** [prohibition] of **Rechiluth** [Gossip] obtains even when the speaker does not intend in his **Rechiluth** [Gossip] to inject hatred into his - the hearer's heart against that man who occasioned the **Rechiluth** [Gossip], and even if, in his - the speaker's opinion, the one who said or did something against him was right - as when **Shimon** reproved **Reuven** for what he said or did to him, and **Reuven** justifies himself, saying that the **Din** [the law] was with him, for Yehuda said the same thing about him - **Shimon** - still if he - **Reuven** believes that because of this, hatred will be aroused in the heart of **Shimon** against Yehuda, he is called a talebearer.

Seif 4

All that we have said about **Rechiluth** [Gossip] being forbidden applies even when it the story is absolutely true, containing no admixture of falsehood. And not only when they have loved each other from the beginning and he - the speaker goes and bears a tale from one against the other, is he called **wicked** and **an abomination before the Lord** - These[4] six are hated by the Lord, and the seventh is the abomination of His soul... and the inciter of strife among brothers, concerning which **Chazal** [Sages] have said - This[5] seventh the inciter of strife is the severest of all. But even if in the absence of this **Rechiluth** [Gossip], they bore great hatred towards each other, and this one - the speaker went and bore the tale, he is called - **a talebearer**.

Seif 5

There is no difference in the **Issur** [prohibition] of speaking **Rechiluth** [Gossip] as to whether he told him - the whole story of his own volition or whether his friend understood a little by himself and implored him to tell him what Ploni [so and so] said before him about him. And even if his father or Rabbi implored him to tell them what **Ploni** [so and so] had said about them, and even if it is only the **Avak** [dust] of **Rechiluth** [Gossip], in any instance, it is forbidden.

Seif 6

And even if he sees that by his not revealing it, he will suffer great loss in his affairs, being under the authority

---

[4] Mishlei 6:16, 19
[5] Vayikra Rabbah, Metzora 16:61

of others, who, when they understand part of the thing, will rise up against him - to compel him, to reveal all and he is afraid of being suspected of collusion with **Ploni** [so and so] and being dismissed from his position and not being able to provide a livelihood for his family - still, it is forbidden to speak **Rechiluth** [Gossip] - as in the case of all the other negative commandments, where he must give up all that he has rather than transgress them, as stated in **Shulchan**[6] **Aruch**, unless in an instance where revelation might remove damages or put an end to the quarrel. But one must not be too hasty to rely upon this **Heter** [a halachic permit], for it entails many qualifications, as we shall explain below[7] at length, the Lord willing, in.

Seif 7

And, especially, if by not telling the story, he will not suffer monetary loss, but only, cursing and reviling, it is certainly forbidden to tell it, and he need not take any note of this at all, knowing in his soul that he will thereby be numbered among the lovers of the Blessed Lord and his face will shine as the light of the sun, as **Chazal** [Sages] have said in the Talmud - Those[8] who are shamed and do not shame in return, who hear themselves reviled and do not answer, etc. About them Scripture writes - But[9] may His friends be as the sun rising in might. How much more so, this one, who suffers humiliation for the Mitzvoth of the Lord[10].

---

[6] Yoreh Deah 157:1
[7] Principle 9
[8] Yoma 23a
[9] Judes 5:31
[10] Hilchoth **Lashon Hara** [slander], Principle 1, section 6

Seif 8

As to answering if one asks him - What did **Ploni** [so and so] say about me? this depends upon the following - If he can answer him in such a way that what he says will not be absolute falsehood nor **Rechiluth** [Gossip], let him answer him in this way and not utter falsehood. But if he understands that his friend will not take this for an answer, he is permitted to utter absolute falsehood for the sake of peace. But he may not swear falsely to this, God forbid[11].

Seif 9

And know that if he does not mention explicitly the name of the man who spoke **Rechiluth** [Gossip] against him, but only speaks in general terms, and afterward, there becomes known to him - the one about whom the story is told, the name of that man, or the specifics of what was said about him - or if he knew by himself what was done to him, but did not know who did it or who spoke against him, and this vendor of **Rechiluth** [Gossip] came and showed him by signs who it was - this, too, is forbidden.

Seif 10

And it is also forbidden to speak **Rechiluth** [Gossip] by deceit. As when one knows that another had caused harm or shame to his friend in the past, and they had quarreled over this, and he now wants to stir up the old quarrel without his - the friend's recognizing this his intent to stir up the quarrel, he contrives with his **slippery lips** to remind him - the friend of the harm or shame caused him by the other in the past, giving him the impression that he

---

[11] see Be'er Mayim Chayim

is talking quite innocently, not knowing who did this to him, whereby the friend remembers by himself who it was - all this, and all like it, is an absolute **Issur** [prohibition].

Seif 11

And know further that there is no difference in the **Issur** [prohibition] of **Rechiluth** [Gossip] as to whether he states explicitly what someone did to him or said about him, or whether he puts it into writing. And it is the same whether he tells him that someone has demeaned him personally or that he has demeaned his wares, since through this - all of the modes, he injects hatred into his heart against him.

CHOFETZ   Part Two   CHAIM

Principle 2

Opening Comments

In this principle, there will be explained the **Din** [the law] of **Rechiluth** [Gossip] in the presence of three, and other details. It contains four sections.

Seif 1
It is forbidden to speak **Rechiluth** [Gossip], even in the presence of one, how much more so, in the presence of many.

Seif 2
Even the **Avak** [dust] of **Rechiluth**[12] [Gossip] is forbidden to be spoken in all instances, even if what he says that **Ploni** [so and so] spoke about the other may be taken in two ways. If he says it in a way that indicates that the intent of **Ploni** [so and so] was to demean him, certainly it is forbidden to mention it, in all instances. And even if the manner in which he expresses it inclines more to the other interpretation of his words, that the intent of **Ploni** [so and so] was not to demean him, still, if he knew the nature of the one spoken about to be that of a **Nirgan** [a grumbler], one who always judges his friend in the scales of guilt, and says of whatever his friend does or speaks that his intent is only to oppose him[13], or if there is, aside from this, a measure of hatred between them from the past, and a man like this is only seeking some

---

[12] Principle 8
[13] S'haarei Teshuvah 231

pretext against his friend, it is forbidden to mention it in any instance.

Seif 3

There are some who say that if one spoke demeaningly of his friend before three, the **Issur** [prohibition] of **Rechiluth** [Gossip] no longer obtains if they go back and say to him - **Ploni** [so and so] spoke this and this **Rechiluth** [Gossip] against you, the reason being that it is something which is bound to be revealed in the end, for **your friend has a friend**, and the Torah did not forbid this by reason of **Rechiluth** [Gossip]. But in this, the qualifications must be observed, which were explained in **Halachoth** [the Law] **Lashon**[14] **Hara** [slander], and on. But one is not to rely on this opinion in practice. For the **M'aharshal**[15] in his commentary on the **S'emag**[16] writes that many of the **Rishonim** [the first Sages ones] dispute this opinion and forbid it, even to tell it to another if he intends to reveal it, and certainly to this one - the one has spoken of himself.

Seif 4

And, according to this, if one wanted to leave his business partner, thinking that others would join in partnership with him, and in the end, this did not materialize - as also a groom from his **Shidduch** [match], it is forbidden to reveal this intention to his first partner, even though the matter had been heard before three or more, as we have written in section 3. Certainly, he the first partner, will

---

[14] Principle 2, section 4
[15] Rabbi Solomon Luria
[16] The Sefer Mitzvot Gadol - Rabbi Moses of Coucy

hold it against his partner for wanting to leave him, as it is written - And[17] why do you come to me **Yiftach** [The judge in those days] now when you are in distress. And this might be cause for the dissolution of their partnership or for the first to distress the second, as the Rambam writes - And[18] if one tells another thing… that lead his friend to be harmed in his body or in his possessions or to be distressed or frightened, this is Lashon Hara [slander].

---

[17] Judges 11:7
[18] Hilchoth Deoth 7:5

Principle 3

Opening Comments

In this principle, it will be explained that the **Issur** [prohibition] of **Rechiluth** [Gossip] obtains both in the object's presence and not in his presence. It contains four sections.

Seif 1
It is forbidden to speak Rechiluth [Gossip] even if it is absolutely true, without admixture of falsehood, even if not before him, the object of the **Rechiluth** [Gossip], and even if he knows in himself that he would say it even to his face, and it is called - **Rechiluth** [Gossip]. Much more so is it forbidden if he has the audacity to tell him to his face - You spoke or did this and this against him. His sin is far greater if he tells him to his face. First, for by telling him to his face he injects great hatred into the heart of the accused against him. For now, it will be accepted by him as absolute truth in that he will say - If it were not absolutely true, he would not dare speak thus to his face. And, furthermore, aside from this, he brings himself and these two to transgress through such **Rechiluth** [Gossip] several explicit negative and positive commandments in the Torah, see[19] the introduction.

Seif 2
If **Reuven** spoke against **Shimon** before **Levi**, and **Levi** went and told this to **Shimon**, it is forbidden for Shimon to say afterward to **Reuven** - How did you speak against me

---
[19] Negative Commandments, Principle 16, and the note thereon

before **Levi**? For in doing so, he - **Shimon**, also transgresses the prohibition of **Rechiluth** [Gossip] because of his mentioning of **Levi**, even if he does not explicitly mention **Levi's** name, but simply says - to **Reuven** - I heard that you said this and this about me - If through this, **Reuven** will naturally understand who revealed it to him, it is forbidden. And in our many sins, many go astray in this.

Seif 3

And know also that it is called **Rechiluth** [Gossip] even if he did not say it before the one it concerns, as when one says to his friend - Such and such did I hear about **Reuven** that he said about **Shimon**. For these words lead, if they are heard, one man from another, to stir up strife between **Reuven**, the speaker, and the one who was spoken about. And one must be careful not to speak of such things. For even if he wants to warn his friend not to reveal this story to anyone, even if he knows for a certainty that he will fulfill his word, it is forbidden for in most cases, there is normally heard at the time of the telling something demeaning about **Reuven** or about Shimon, and it does not leave the category of **Lashon Hara** [slander]. And much more is it forbidden to tell him what **Ploni** [so and so] spoke against his sons or relatives, for it is a man's nature to be aggrieved by this, and it is called - **Rechiluth** [Gossip].

Seif 4

And if it were his intent in relating this to his friend to have him rebuke **Reuven** for speaking **Lashon Hara** [slander] against Shimon, see above[20].

---

[20] Part One, Principle 10, section 6

CHOFETZ — Part Two — CHAIM

Principle 4

Opening Comments

In this principle there will be explained the **Din** [the law] of **Rechiluth** [Gossip] in an instance where the thing itself is known to him without the story, and how to correct this sin.

Seif 1

The **Issur** [prohibition] of **Rechiluth** [Gossip] obtains even if he does not reveal to him anything new, he himself knowing that thus and thus did **Ploni** [so and so] speak about him or that he did this and this thing that affected him, but he did not yet reflect upon whether **Ploni** [so and so] wronged him thereby, and this talebearer reminds him of this. As when **Reuven** left the **Beth-Din** [Court] liable in the judgment, and **Shimon** met him and asked him - What happened with your case? And **Reuven** answered - I was found liable for this and this, whereupon **Shimon** said - They did not judge you correctly, and the like. Even so, this is called **Rechiluth** [Gossip] for by his speaking, a new perspective is created which leads to implanting hatred in his heart against **Ploni** [so and so].

Seif 2

If Reuven demeaned **Shimon** before two, and one of them transgressed the **Issur** [prohibition] of **Rechiluth** [Gossip] and revealed the thing to Shimon, still, the second should take care not to reveal it to Shimon, how much more so, if he **enforces** the account, and he is called a talebearer because of this. And not only is it forbidden if he understands from **Shimon** that he is still in doubt about the veracity of the thing - as when **Shimon** asks him - Is it true what your friend told me, that **Reuven** demeaned me before you? in which case it is certainly forbidden to tell him, but even without this he should not tell him, for by his words he intensifies **Shimon** hatred against **Reuven**, the story being more greatly emphasized if he hears it from two than if he hears if only from one. And sometimes they - **Reuven** and **Shimon** will come to quarrel because of this second one, who re-arouses the **Rechiluth** [Gossip].

Seif 3
And if he transgressed and spoke **Rechiluth** [Gossip] against his friend and came to repent for his sin, there is no amendment for him until he asks forgiveness of him and conciliates him. And he must also repent to his Maker for having transgressed - You[21] shall not go **Rachil** [talebearing] among your people. And all the details of his **Din** [the law] are the same as in the instance of **Lashon Hara** [slander] see above[22].

---

[21] Leviticus 19:16
[22] Part One, Principle 4, section 2

CHOFETZ — Part Two — CHAIM

Principle 5

Opening Comments

In this principle, there will be explained the **Issur** [prohibition] of accepting **Rechiluth** [Gossip] and of hearing it, in all of its details. And, also, if he transgresses, how to atone for this sin? It contains seven sections.

Seif 1

Just as it is forbidden to accept **Lashon Hara** [slander], according to the Torah, so is it forbidden to accept **Rechiluth** [Gossip] according to the Torah, it, too, being in the category of **Lashon Hara** [slander]. That is, he must not believe in his heart that what was told him about **Ploni** [so and so] having done to him or said about him is true. And the accepter transgresses - You[23] shall not bear a false report. aside from the other negative and positive commandments - **Lashon**[24] **Hara** [slander] kills three - the speaker, the accepter, and the one it was said about. As we know from the episode of **Doeg**, who was banished from the world to come because of speaking **Rechiluth** [Gossip], and Nov the city of Cohanim was wiped out because of the **Rechiluth** [Gossip] spoken about them, and Saul was killed thereafter because of having accepted the **Rechiluth** [Gossip]. And the accepter is worse than the speaker. And **Chazal** [Sages] have said in the Talmud - That[25] if one speaks **Lashon Hara** [slander] or accepts

---

[23] Shemoth 23:1
[24] Arachin 15b
[25] Pesachim 118a

CHOFETZ   Part Two   CHAIM

Lashon Hara [slander], he is fit to be cast to the dogs, it is written - You[26] shall not bear a false report, preceded by - To[27] the dog shall you cast it.

Seif 2
And even for listening to **Rechiluth** [Gossip] alone there is also a great **Issur** [prohibition], as in the case of **Lashon Hara** [slander] see above[28], even if at the time of listening he has not yet decided to believe or not. But, in any event, the **Issur** [prohibition] of acceptance is more severe than that of listening. For as far as listening is concerned, if he understands from the beginning of the story that knowing this thing will affect him in the future if it is true, as when he sees that his friend wants to tell him that **Ploni** [so and so] wants to harm him in his body or in his possessions, and the like, it is certainly permitted to listen in the beginning to know how to take care and guard himself against him. But to accept it categorically is forbidden by the Torah in all instances, and he is permitted only to suspect, in order to take care to guard himself, as **Chazal** [Sages] have said about **Lashon Hara** [slander], that even though one should not accept it, he should suspect it. And see above[29], **Halachoth** [the Law] **Issurei** [prohibition] **Lashon Hara** [slander], on how to conduct oneself with respect to listening, in order to satisfy the obligation of Heaven in respect to listening. The **Din** [the law] is the same here.

Seif 3
And if he sees in his friend indications that he wishes to

---

[26] Shemot 22:29
[27] Shemot 22:3
[28] Principle 6 Part One, Principle 6, section 2
[29] Principle 6

harm him in his body or in his possessions, even if he did not hear such a thing from anyone until this point, he is permitted to make inquiries of others as to whether he intends to harm him in this and this matter in order to know how to protect himself from him. And he need not fear that by doing so he might cause people to speak demeaningly of that man.

Seif 4

And know further that all of the principles that we wrote about above[30], concerning **Lashon Hara** [slander], regarding suspecting apply here in the area of **Rechiluth** [Gossip]. Therefore, one must be very careful, when he hears that someone has spoken about him or done this and this to him or wants to do this and this to him, not to believe it, but only to suspect, that is, to guard himself against him. And not by way of doubt, for we assume a man to be in a status of **Kashruth** [Kosher], and that in all probability he has not harmed him or demeaned him. It is, therefore, forbidden to do anything against him or to cause him any harm or shame because of this, large or small. And it is even forbidden to hate him in one's heart according to the Torah. How much more so is it forbidden not to exempt oneself because of the **Rechiluth** [Gossip] from any obligation one has to the suspected? And he is still obligated to accord him all the benefits commanded by the Torah to other men in Israel. For his worth has not diminished in our eyes through this in any respect. And, as a general rule, the **Poskim** [Halachic Rulings] has written that it is not permitted to suspect except where it concerns one's future safety, that he not come to harm

---

[30] Part One, Principle 6

because of him. But in any other area, it is forbidden to suspect at all.

Seif 5

And from this, you will see how foolish those many people whose nature it is always to ask their friends what others have said about them, even if they know that this makes no difference to them in the future. And when they do not want to reveal it, they implore them until they reveal what **Ploni** [so and so] has said about them. And in their reply, there are some demeaning things that were said about them. And they accept this report as the absolute truth - and, as a result, they become absolute haters. Now if we come to weigh the greatness of the harm and to count the number of negative and positive commandments likely to be transgressed by one possessed of this degrading nature, the sheet is too short to contain them - See the introduction and you will understand our words. For, in truth, the **Issur** [prohibition] of accepting **Lashon Hara** [slander] and **Rechiluth** [Gossip] obtains even if one tells him of his own volition something that affects him in the future. The Torah commands not to believe but only to suspect. And when it does not affect him in the future, even listening alone is forbidden as mentioned above[31]. How much more so is it forbidden to stand over his friend and beg him to tell, until the speaker becomes a speaker of **Rechiluth** [Gossip], and the listener, an accepter of **Rechiluth** [Gossip], so that he is a sinner and he causes his friend to sin. Therefore, one must distance himself greatly from inquiring about such a thing, unless it is clear to him that

---

[31] section 2

he must know it for his future welfare to know how to guard himself against **Ploni** [so and so].

Seif 6

And know that there is yet another aspect of the **Issur** [prohibition] of accepting **Rechiluth** [Gossip], as I shall explain. For even if it is clear to him that what was told him is true, that one spoke or did something against his will, still, he must be judged in the scales of good and merit, that his intent in this was not to antagonize him, but something else, which, if understood on its own terms, would not be considered a wrong against him. And it is well known that it is a Mitzvah according to the **Din** [the law] to judge one on the scales of merit. And he, because he did not want to judge him on the scales of merit, came to see what the other did as wrong, and held it against him in his heart because of this. Therefore, he is called because of this - an accepter of **Rechiluth** [Gossip].

Seif 7

And if he already transgressed and accepted **Rechiluth** [Gossip], his amendment is to strengthen himself to remove this thing from his heart and not believe it. And even if it is difficult for him to believe that the speaker invented the whole thing, let him think that he added to or detracted from, some details of the act, or some words of the speech that **Ploni** [so and so] attributed to him, or that he related it in a different intonation that turned it from good to bad. And let him accept upon himself for the future never again to accept **Lashon Hara** [slander] or **Rechiluth** [Gossip] against any Jew, and let him confess his sin. And he will thereby correct the **Issur** [prohibition] that he transgressed if he has not yet told the thing to others.

CHOFETZ — Part Two — CHAIM

Principle 6

Opening Comments

In this principle, there will be explained the **Issur** [prohibition] of accepting **Rechiluth** [Gossip] if stated before three or before him, and the **Din** [the law], if he suffered harm and a rumor went forth that **Ploni** [so and so] caused him this harm, or if one spoke to him **innocently** of this, or if he were told by one whom he believes like two witnesses and other details of the **Din** [the law] of **Rechiluth** [Gossip]. It contains ten sections.

Seif 1
It is forbidden to accept **Rechiluth** [Gossip], even if the speaker said the thing in public before many men. For even if he did so, it is not to be concluded because of this that what he says is true. But it is to be suspected as possibly true and inquired about if it may affect him in the future.

Seif 2
Just as we explained above[32] that according to the **Din** [the law], it is forbidden to accept **Lashon Hara** [slander], even if he spoke it to his face, so is it with **Rechiluth** [Gossip]. That is if one said to his face - You said this and this about him, even if he remains silent now when the **Rechiluth** [Gossip] is spoken about him, it is still forbidden to accept it, and no proof is to be derived from this his silence that the thing is true. And even if it is the

---

[32] Part One, Principle 6, section 2

nature of that man not to remain silent in other matters, and he does so here, still, this is no proof of the truth of the matter, as we explained above. And, all of this, even if the talebearer does not transgress, in what he says - You[33] shall not go **Rachil** [talebearing] among your people. As when he tells him to guard himself against **Ploni** [so and so], who wants to harm him, and the like, as we shall explain below. How much more so, if he speaks about him words of Lashon Hara [slander] and **Rechiluth** [Gossip] in general? Have we not already explained above, in the name of the **Poskim** [Halachic Rulings] that **Lashon Hara** [slander] and **Rechiluth** [Gossip] are forbidden, whether in his presence or not? If so, even if all is true, as he says, that **Ploni** [so and so] said this and this about him, still, he - the speaker is an absolute evildoer, according to his tale itself, for he transgresses the negative commandment of - You shall not go **Rachil** [talebearing] among your people. And the other negative and positive commandments are explained above in the introduction. And, if so, because of this evildoer, shall we remove this man the one spoken against from his status of **Kashruth** [Kosher] and say that he transgressed the **Issur** [prohibition] of **Lashon Hara** [slander] and the like? Certainly, one who is suspected of transgressing the negative commandment of **Rechiluth** [Gossip] and **Lashon Hara** [slander] is also suspected of lying and adding words, and changing things from beginning to end.

Seif 3

And if he suffered a business loss and did not know its

---

[33] Vayikra 19:17

cause, as when he held a lease from a landowner and was dismissed by him, and he did not know whether someone had slandered him or whether the landowner had dismissed him at his own initiative it is forbidden to suspect a Jew unless there are **indications** pointing to him as will be explained below, in which instance he is permitted to believe the **Rechiluth** [Gossip] in his heart, but he is not permitted to cause him the suspect any loss thereby as will be explained below. For it is forbidden to categorize a Jew as an **evildoer**. And concerning this it is said - In[34] the scales of righteousness shall you judge your fellow. And even if he heard that **Ploni** [so and so] caused him the loss, still, he is permitted only to suspect, but not to confirm it within himself as being true. And even if people stirred up a quarrel with the suspect, telling him that he had done a great wrong in what was heard of him, that he had caused a loss to a Jew - and he kept quiet, still, it is not to be concluded because of this that the thing is true. For though it is a Mitzvah for him to rescue himself from suspicion and to convince the one who suspected him that he is not to be suspected, as per - And[35] you shall be clean of guilt against the Lord and against Israel, still, it may be that he saw them be so entrenched in their acceptance of the slander as being true, that they would accept no answer from him, wherefore he decided that it would be best for him to remain silent and to be one of those - who are shamed but do not shame in return, who hear their disgrace and do not answer.

Seif 4

And know further that the **Issur** [prohibition] of the acceptance of **Rechiluth** [Gossip] obtains even if he

---

[34] Vayikra 19:15
[35] Bamidbar 32:22

heard from two or more, or it was rumored in the city, that **Ploni** [so and so] spoke against him or did this and this to him. Still, it is forbidden to accept this and to confirm the thing in his heart as being true, even if the intent of the speakers, according to their words, was for his future good. Jews are not rendered **evildoers** because of their - the speaker's words as mentioned above[36].

Seif 5

The **Issur** [prohibition] of accepting **Rechiluth** [Gossip] obtains even when the speaker is believed by him as two witnesses, and even if there were in that thing the **Rechiluth** [Gossip] no possibility of a **scale of merit** interpretation. All this, when there is no future benefit in his knowing this thing. But if there is, as when he is told that **Ploni** [so and so] wants to harm him in his body or his possessions and the like, so that he can guard himself against him, it is permitted to accept this from him and to believe it. But he may not reveal it to others, even to the members of his household, unless this revelation may be of future benefit. And all this, if he was told - by the speaker, that he heard this from him - the suspected one, himself. But if he heard it from another who said that he heard it from him, he has no more advantage in credibility than any other man.

Seif 6

And even if there is a prospect of future benefit, this - that he may accept the **Rechiluth** [Gossip], applies only when he knows the man very well, that is when he knows intimately the nature of that man - that he never lies and

---

[36] Section 2

that he never omits things. For this reason, he relies upon him implicitly, so that his words are always believed in this instance as in all other instances, just as the words of two witnesses who testify in **Beth-Din** [Court], where there is no doubt as to the truth of their testimony. But if in other things he does not believe him that much, but only in this, because tidbits of **Lashon Hara** [slander] and **Rechiluth** [Gossip] are pleasing to his palate, wherefore he resolves within himself that he believes him as two, it is certainly forbidden - to believe him. For the more he believes the thing to be true, the more he enters the class of an accepter of **Rechiluth** [Gossip] and **Lashon Hara** [slander].

Seif 7

And all of this applied in the time of the Talmud, but today, according to the consensus of the **Poskim** [Halachic Rulings], one is not to say - I believe that man like two witnesses that do not lie. It is forbidden to accept his words in any instance, but only to suspect. And even without this, it is not common that all of the conditions mentioned in sections 5 and 7 are met. And from this, you can see how many people err in this matter. They are heedful of the **Issur** [prohibition] of speaking and of accepting **Lashon Hara** [slander] and **Rechiluth** [Gossip] if they hear it from others, but not if they hear it from their fathers or mothers or wives, feeling that these certainly would not lie to them. And this is an absolute mistake, for there is no difference between this and other instances.

Seif 8

The **Din** [the law] of the **Issur** [prohibition] of accepting **Rechiluth** [Gossip] obtains even when he speaks - in his innocence. That is, when he the hearer sees that the speaker did not intend to stir up strife against his friend, but that it the **Rechiluth** [Gossip] left his mouth by chance. All of its other details are explained above[37], in respect to **Lashon Hara** [slander]. The same applies to **Rechiluth** [Gossip].

Seif 9

As far as **indications** are concerned, by which it is seen that what was related to him about **Ploni** [so and so], as having done or said this and this to him is true - whether or not to believe what was said - see above[38], where we explained, with the Lord's help, all the relevant details. But, in order to make the reading easier, I shall set down what emerges from there - that the following conditions must be met -

> **A.** that there not be in the **indications** of the truth of the **Rechiluth** [Gossip] anything to judge him in the scales of merit. For if not - That is, if there were something which suggested judging him in the scales of merit, how are **indications of the truth** of the **Rechiluth** [Gossip] relevant here? Even if the **Rechiluth** [Gossip] is true, it is not to be believed about the suspect that he intended wrong thereby, as mentioned above in several places.
>
> **B.** that it be an actual **indication**, that relates to the story, and not a slight **indication**.
>
> **C.** that he sees the **indications** himself, and does not hear of them from others.

---

[37] Part One, Principle 7, section 9
[38] Part One, Principle 7, sections 10-14

> **D.** that there might be some future benefit in knowing the story, failing which, it is forbidden to incline one's ear and listen to it, as we wrote in several places.
>
> **E.** After all this, indications are of avail only as far as believing the story in his heart, but not to go and publicize it to others. In any event, it is forbidden to rely upon actual **indications** to cause him monetary loss or to strike him, God forbid, see above[39], where we expanded on this.

Seif 10

And through this, you will see in actuality how far we have gone astray in our many sins - that if one suffers a loss through an informer or the like, and he has **indications** against a Jew, relying upon them - the indications, he goes and informs against him too. For it is an axiom among people that if one informed on his friend, the latter may inform on him too. And, in truth, this is an absolute error for several reasons -

> **A.** This is only if the second informing may lead to future benefit, that his antagonist does not repeat his informing. If he cannot rescue himself in any other way, this is permitted. But if his intent is only to avenge himself upon him, it is certainly an absolute **Issur** [prohibition] as explained in **Shulchan**[40] **Aruch**.
>
> **B.** Furthermore, all of this applies only if he saw himself being informed against with his own eyes, but he may not rely on **indications**, even if they are

---

[39] Section 14
[40] Choshen Mishpat 388:9

real indications and he saw them himself. How much more so is it forbidden [to accept the **Rechiluth** [Gossip] if he were told by others that he had informed against him? For in such an instance, even to believe in his heart that the thing is true is also forbidden, so long as they have not testified against him in **Beth-Din** [Court] or even outside of **Beth-Din** [Court] if it is absolutely clear that there is no doubt about the story. How much more so is it forbidden to rely upon this and to cause his friend any monetary loss, even if his intent in this is **future benefit**.

CHOFETZ — Part Two — CHAIM

Principle 7

Opening Comments

In this principle, there will be explained the Issur [prohibition] of speaking **Rechiluth** [Gossip] in all of its aspects. It contains five sections.

Seif 1

There is no difference in the **Issur** [prohibition] of speaking **Rechiluth** [Gossip] as to whether the speaker is a man or a woman, a relative or a stranger. And even if one heard someone speaking demeaningly of his father and mother, and because of his great distress for their honor he revealed it to them, this, too, is in the category of **Rechiluth** [Gossip]. There is also no difference as to whether the one spoken about is a man or a woman, adult or minor as we explained above[41]. And there are people who go astray in this so that if one sees two boys fighting, he goes and tells one of the fathers that the other boy hit his son. And this often results in great damage. The father of this boy, in his hatred, hits the second child, and this results in heated quarreling between the fathers. This most often occurs in the synagogue. Now if we came to reckon the number of **Issurim** [prohibitions] that resulted from this **Rachil** [talebearing], there would be too many to count. And this is so even if he does not know clearly who is right, in which instance it is forbidden to tell the father of either one of them. But even if he does know that one of them is right, in spite of this, he may not tell

---

[41] Part One, Principle 7, sections 1-3

the father of the second, unless the conditions explained below[42].

Seif 2

And know that the **Issur** [prohibition] of **Rechiluth** [Gossip] obtains even if spoken against an **Am Ha'aretz** [ignoramus], he, too, being in the category of **your people**. And even if one sees clearly that this **Am Ha'aretz** [ignoramus] demeaned someone, not to his face, in vain, and that the **Din** [the law] is with the other, still, have we not explained above[43] that the **Issur** [prohibition] of **Rechiluth** [Gossip] obtains even if spoken truthfully? How much greater and more severe is the sin of speaking **Rechiluth** [Gossip] against a Torah scholar, for several reasons -

> **A.** because of the **Rechiluth** [Gossip] itself. For is it not obvious that even if in the **Rechiluth** [Gossip] that he spoke against his friend there were an admixture of falsehood, certainly his punishment is more severe than if it were completely true? And if we look into our instance, it will be found, in most cases to be a **Rechiluth** [Gossip] of falsehood. For a Torah scholar - it may be assumed - does not demean or do wrong to a man in vain, and it may be assumed that what he did, he did according to the **Din** [the law]. Therefore, if one goes and speaks of him as having done something wrong, that is a **Rechiluth** [Gossip] of falsehood.
>
> **B.** because of the very nature of that man - the

---

[42] Principle 9 are satisfied
[43] Principle 1

Torah scholar. For the Torah has commanded us to cleave to them - Torah scholars in all connections - to eat and drink and do business with a Torah scholar, and to marry his daughter to a Torah scholar, and to honor them greatly. How much more so is it forbidden to stir up strife with them? This leads to the opposite of all these.

C. because of what results from this tale. For it is well known that one is not so greatly affected if an **Am Ha'aretz** [ignoramus] demeans him or does him some wrong. But if one is told that a Torah scholar demeaned him, certainly more hatred will enter his heart against him, and it is very likely that strife will be stirred up because of this. And especially if he speaks against the Rabbi of the city, great harm can result from this, and quite often his very livelihood is endangered because of this.

Seif 3

And know further that there is no difference in the **Issur** [prohibition] of **Rechiluth** [Gossip] as to whether he told **Reuven** himself what **Ploni** [so and so] said against him or whether he related this thing to **Reuven's** wife or his relatives. For certainly it will be taken ill by them, and they will hold it against **Ploni** [so and so]. Therefore, even if he exhorted them not to tell this to anyone, the thing does not leave the category of **Rechiluth** [Gossip].

Seif 4

There is also no difference in the **Issur** [prohibition] of **Rechiluth** [Gossip] as to whether he speaks it to a Jew against a Jew or whether he speaks it against a Jew before gentiles. And when we look into it closely, we will find that his sin is much greater in this - the latter, than in **Rechiluth** [Gossip] in general. For in telling him - the gentile what **Ploni** [so and so] the Jew did to him or said about him, he certainly can cause him **Ploni** [so and so] harm and grief. And there are other reasons, as we explained at length above[44]. And there are men who go greatly astray in this, imputing before a gentile a defect in wares sold to him by a Jew, or in work done for him - the gentile, by a Jew, and the like. He thereby may cause the Jew harm and grief, and very often his very livelihood is endangered thereby.

Seif 5
As far as the **Issur** [prohibition] of acceptance of **Rechiluth** [Gossip] is concerned, its **Din** [the law] is like that of **Lashon Hara** [slander] as stated above[45]. Therefore, one should take great care not to accept **Rechiluth** [Gossip] from anyone, even his wife. And when we look into this, we find that in accepting **Rechiluth** [Gossip] from his wife in her saying that **Ploni** [so and so] spoke thus and thus about him, aside from the sin itself of acceptance of **Rechiluth** [Gossip], he brings many troubles upon himself. For when she sees that her husband accepts the words graciously, she will always relate such things to him, and bring him thereby to strife, contention, and dejection. Therefore, it is fitting that **a man of spirit** rebukes his wife when she tells him such things.

---

[44] Part One, Principle 8, section 12
[45] Part One, Principle 8, sections 2 and 4

CHOFETZ   Part Two   CHAIM

Principle 8

Opening Comments

In this principle, there will be explained the **Avak** [dust] of **Rechiluth** [Gossip] in all of its aspects. It contains five sections.

Seif 1
There are many things which are forbidden because of the **Avak** [dust] of **Rechiluth** [Gossip]. I shall explain some of them in short, and the intelligent reader will infer their parallels - one's telling his friend that they asked **Ploni** [so and so] about him and he answered - Hush. I do not want to mention what happened and what is going to happen. All such things, where one tells him how **Ploni's** [so and so] words intimated something ill of him are in the category of the **Avak** [dust] of slander.

Seif 2
And so, if one praises another before him - the other's friend, where such praise can raise resentment in his - the friend's heart against him - the other, and harm may result, this is in the category of the **Avak** [dust] of **Rechiluth** [Gossip]. Therefore, it seems to me that one should take care not to praise **Reuven** before **Shimon**, his partner - or a woman before her husband or a husband before his wife, for having granted him a loan or given him charity or paying him well for his work, and the like. This might arouse resentment in the heart of **Shimon** against his partner **Reuven** - for having overextended

himself. And sometimes this might lead to harm to **Reuven** or to quarreling and thus a husband vis-a-vis his wife, **Shimon** thinking that **Reuven** was extravagant in his expenditures.

Seif 3
And thus, one must take care, when he asks his friend for a favor and the other declines, not to ask him - Why did you do this for **Ploni** [so and so]? He himself told me - for this is also likely to arouse the friend's resentment against **Ploni** [so and so] for having revealed the thing to others, whom he now cannot refuse.

Seif 4
And there are other things which are forbidden because of the **Avak** [dust] of **Rechiluth** [Gossip], such as revealing to another what someone said about him, which, though not demeaning, most men would object to having repeated before him.

Seif 5
And a man must conceal a secret which his friend tells him in private, even though there is no **Rechiluth** [Gossip] in the revelation of this secret. For there is in its revelation harm to its confider and cause for voidance of his plans. Also, in this - **Avak** [dust] of **Rechiluth** [Gossip], he departs from the way of modesty and transgresses the will of his confidant.

CHOFETZ   Part Two   CHAIM

Principle 9

Opening Comments

In this principle, there will be explained situations where the **Issur** [prohibition] of **Rechiluth** [Gossip] does not obtain if the necessary conditions are met. It contains fifteen sections.
Above, in the **Halachoth** [the Law] of the **Issurim** [prohibitions] of **Lashon Hara** [slander], see below[46], we explained how **Lashon Hara** [slander] may be spoken if one conducted himself improperly in matters **between man and his neighbor**, where the intent of the speaker is for benefit alone. And now, in this principle, we shall explain how **Rechiluth** [Gossip] may be spoken ab initio if the speaker intends to remove possible harm. And I pray to the Lord that I do not stumble in a matter of **Halacha** [the Law].

Seif 1
If one sees that his friend wishes to enter into partnership with someone, and he feels that he will certainly be harmed by this, he must tell him to rescue him from that harm, but the following five conditions must be met -

Seif 2
They are -
> **A.** He must be careful not to immediately conclude that harm will result but must reflect carefully from the beginning to see if the result will, indeed, be

---

[46] Part One, Principle 8, section 12

harmful.

B. He must not exaggerate the matter to be worse than it actually is.

C. His intent must be for benefit only, that is, to remove the harm from the first, and not because he hates the other. And in this third condition, we shall include yet another matter - that aside from his intending benefit and not being motivated by hatred, he must first reflect as to whether the benefit will actually sprout from this - as opposed to what happens very often, that even if tells him, he will not listen to him but will enter into partnership with him, and afterward when his partner angers him with something, he will tell him - **He was right when he told me not to become your partner**, and the like. For such people, whom he recognizes to possess this evil trait of **Rechiluth** [Gossip], no **Heter** [a halachic permit] is conceivable, for it makes these blind men stumble in the absolute negative commandment of **Rechiluth** [Gossip].

D. If he can affect this benefit in some other way without having to speak badly of the other, he should do so.

E. All this is permitted only if absolute harm will not come to the one spoken of because of what is said about him. That is, they are not permitted to do him any positive harm, but only to deprive him of the good that might have come to him from the partnership. Even though even this is bad for him, in any event, it is permitted. But if absolute harm comes to him because of what is said about him, it is forbidden to speak about him, for this would require other conditions, as will be explained below, the Lord willing, in sections 5 and 6. And how much more so is it forbidden if he sees that his story would cause the subject great harm, more than the **Din** [the law] prescribes, as stated in below[47].

Seif 3

And now we shall describe another situation where the **Issur** [prohibition] of **Rechiluth** [Gossip] does not obtain. If one heard another saying - If I meet **Ploni** [so and so] in this and this place, I will beat him or I will insult and shame him, or if he heard from him that he intends to cause him monetary loss, the **Din** [the law] depends on this - If this man has a reputation for such things, having actually done such things many times to other persons, or if he the observer recognizes according to the situation that what left his mouth was not a sheer exaggeration and that he would actually act upon his words, he must reveal this to the other party. Perhaps he would be able to take heed of the other so that he not be shamed or harmed by him. But here, too, he must take care that all of the above conditions are not lacking.

Seif 4

And even though this thing - That is, to reveal it when necessary, is a great Mitzvah and in the category of **fostering peace**, still, great care must be taken not to hasten to reveal such a thing except if, after reflecting upon the matter, he knows that the hearer will take care

---

[47] Section 5

not to go to that place alone, lest he be beaten or insulted by that man, or follow some other counsel of this kind, whereby the quarrel between them may be terminated. For very often it happens that if one tells someone that **Ploni** [so and so] intends to insult him, he grows even angrier with him, and actually puts himself in his way to quarrel with him. The revealer, therefore, might cause even greater strife, God forbid, so that he must think very carefully, in the beginning, how to rectify things.

Seif 5

And now we come to explain with the help of the Blessed Lord, yet another great principle in these things, by which the fifth condition will also be clarified for you. Know that the entire **Heter** [a halachic permit] that we wrote about[48] - obtains only if the man to whom he would reveal the story did not yet consummate the partnership with the other, but only agreed to do so. But if it were consummated - by each according to his circumstances, as explained by the **Poskim** [Halachic Rulings], in such a manner as to forbid their retraction thereafter, the **Din** [the law] depends in this - if he - the prospective revealer knows that by revealing what he knows about the man, the other would harm him in no way, but only guard himself so that from now on no harm would befall him, and all the conditions set down[49] - were also met, then it would be proper to do so. That is, to reveal it. But if he knew the nature of the man to whom he would tell it, to be such that as soon as he heard it he would believe it implicitly - either because it is his nature to believe such

---

[48] Section 1
[49] Section 2

things immediately of his neighbor, or because there are **indications** - pointing to the truth of the revelation, or because he relies on him the teller implicitly, and he would immediately rule for himself and take action, That is, withdraw from his agreement or do him some other injury, then even if he would not do anything worse than the **Din** [the law] that **Beth-Din** [Court] would pronounce if two witnesses testified in **Beth-Din** [Court] according to his - the revealer's words, still, it is forbidden to reveal it. For by his revealing, it he does harm to the man [he speaks about], as would not be the case even if he testified about him in **Beth-Din** [Court]. For even if he said the very same thing in **Beth-Din** [Court]. **Beth-Din** [Court] could not impose upon him monetary payment according to his testimony, his being a single witness, whose testimony is not accepted. And now if he revealed it, he would cause him real harm by doing so. And, according to this, if the tellers of the thing were two, who themselves witnessed it, it would seem to be permitted for them to reveal it. For their intent is only to rescue the hearer from harm and also not to cause the other, by their revelation, more than accords with the **Din** [the law]. For if they see that by revealing it, he the **Heter** [a halachic permit] would cause the other harm, which even **Beth-Din** [Court] would not impose upon their testimony, they have no advantage over a single witness, and it certainly would be forbidden for them to reveal it. And it is also necessary to ensure that none of the other particulars mentioned above[50] are lacking.

---

[50] section 2

Seif 6

But this entire **Heter** [a halachic permit] of two witnesses in the case of a man who is likely **to rule for himself** is of avail only to rescue them from the **Issur** [prohibition] of forbidden speech, but, in any case, they do not thereby leave the class of **abettors to the committers of transgression.** For through them, the hearer will most likely do something forbidden. For according to the **Din** [the law] it is forbidden for him to accept their words and do something himself to cause loss to his friend so long as they have not testified in **Beth-Din** [Court] and **Beth-Din** [Court] have allowed him to do this, as explained above[51] . Aside from this, it is very difficult to conceive of this **Din** [the law] arising in reality, to permit it in this case - aside from the fact that it is very rare for all of the necessary conditions to coincide. For it is hard to be found that those who speak by themselves and not in **Beth-Din** [Court] know in the beginning all the aspects of the **Dinim** [the law] in such an instance so as to assess that what **Ploni** [so and so] will do to him because of their speaking will accord with the **Din** [the law] of the Torah. Therefore, care must be taken not to reveal anything to a man whose nature is to **rule for himself** without the permission of **Beth-Din** [Court], so that they not be entrapped through him in the snare of **the men of the tongue.** And - He[52] who guards his mouth and his tongue guards his soul from distress.

Seif 7

The same is true of revealing to another that **Ploni** [so and

---

[51] Principle 6, sections 9 and 10
[52] Proverbs 21:23

so] has robbed or harmed him, or the like. This is not permitted unless all the aforementioned conditions are met and he reproved him the thief, etc. in the beginning and his reproof was not accepted. But without this, it is forbidden see above[53]. And how much must one take heed, not to give himself a **Heter** [a halachic permit] immediately in these things, until he has reflected carefully in the beginning if all the conditions have been met? For it not so, he is very likely to transgress the absolute negative transgression of **Rechiluth** [Gossip].

Seif 8
And know that there is no difference in this principle as to whether his friend asks him to tell him, or whether to tell him himself. For if all the conditions in this principle have been met, even if he asks nothing of him, he must tell him, and if not, it is forbidden in all cases.

Seif 9
And know further, that he must be heedful of all the particulars of this principle even if he wishes to tell only others. This too, is in the category of **Rechiluth** [Gossip], as we wrote above[54] in this part.

Seif 10
And since it is very easy to stray into **Rechiluth** [Gossip] in this matter, we shall have to illustrate this with several examples and expand upon them, so that the intelligent reader draws parallels to all that is like this. But so that the reader not tire of their length, I shall give here only

---

[53] Principle 1, section 3
[54] Principle 3, section 3

one illustration, and if the Lord wills it, I shall add some more at the end of the book. If he sees that a man wants to enter a store to buy something, and he knows that man to be rather naïve, and he knows the shopkeeper to be a man whose entire yearning is to ensnare a man like that and deceive him - whether in matters of weights and measures or in bargaining - he must tell him about that store and warn him not to enter it, even if he has already agreed with that storekeeper to buy from him. How much more so if he sees clearly that the storekeeper wishes to deceive him as to the merchandise? That is, to convince him that he is buying the very best quality, when he knows this to be false, or in the area of weights and measures or in the purchase price. In such cases, he must certainly tell him, so that he not come to be deceived. But he must take great care that the aforementioned conditions, as stated above[55] are satisfied.

Seif 11

All this, if he wishes to warn him against being cheated. But if he already has bought merchandise from someone and he knows that he cheated him in the purchase price or in other areas, the **Din** [the law] in this instance is dependent upon the following - If, according to the **Din** [the law] of the Torah, he now has no claim against the storekeeper - as when the overcharge was less than one-sixth, or if the allotted time has passed for him to show it to a merchant or to his relative, or for any other reason that the one cheated sustains the loss, then certainly, if one goes and brings this to the attention of the cheated one, and shows him how **Ploni** [so and so] has cheated

---

[55] Section 2

him, he transgresses the **Issur** [prohibition] of **Rechiluth** [Gossip]. For since, according to the **Din** [the law] of the Torah, he now has no claim against him, then the telling of this is only talk in general, and he the teller is like the proverbial peddler, who peddles things from one to the other. And even if the cheated one asks him to tell, he should not tell him the truth. How much more so, if he sees that through his speaking the storekeeper can suffer a loss, such as being caught by the authorities or not being paid what is still owed him for this transaction. Certainly, the one who brings this about. That is, the teller - is guilty of a great sin. But if he sees that according to the Torah, the **Din** [the law] is with him - then he may back out of the transaction or receive the amount of the overcharge. And if he knew that if the cheated one knew this, he would not acquiesce in the transaction, then he must tell him the truth as it is, in order to recover the money from the merchant. But he must be heedful of the following -

Seif 12

    A. He must not exaggerate the wrong or the loss beyond what it is.

    B. His prime intent must be to be zealous for the truth and to help him that has been wronged That is, the cheated one. And he must not rejoice in the shame of the cheater, even though he knows clearly that he cheated him. And in this connection, we shall include yet another detail, that is almost the same as the original. That is, in order to tell he must assume that benefit will result - as opposed to an instance where he knows the nature of the cheated one not to be a man of words who would go to judgment and ask people to help him in this matter, but would only grieve in his heart at the story and harbor hatred in his heart against the merchant. In such an instance he should not tell him. Even more, if he asks him to tell in this instance and in the previous instance that we described - that is, in an instance where, according to the **Din** [the law], it is forbidden to back out of the transaction, it is a Mitzvah to praise the purchase before him, and he does not thereby transgress - From[56] a thing of falsehood shall you keep far. As **Chazal** [Sages] have said in the Talmud - If[57] one made a bad purchase in the marketplace - he should praise it in his eyes.

C. If he feels that his words of reproof will be heard by the merchant to return the overcharge, then he should reprove him between themselves to return it, and not reveal it to the purchaser.

D. If he can bring about the benefit by other means, where he need not demean him, he should not tell it.

E. The man that he tells must not be by his nature a talebearer. If he knows him to possess this base trait, and that he probably will tell the merchant - **Ploni** [so and so] told me that this merchandise is defective, or that it is not worth what he paid for it, this requires looking into - whether it is permitted to tell a man like this the truth, for he may cause him to stumble into the **Issur** [prohibition] of **Rechiluth** [Gossip]. In any event, it seems that if

---

[56] Shemoth 23:7
[57] Kethuvoth 17a

he feels that if he exhorts him not to reveal his name, he will be heeded, he should tell him.

Seif 13

All that we have said applies if he knows the nature of the cheated one to be such that if the truth of the cheating is made known to him, he will not do anything by himself, but will summon him to **Beth-Din** [Court] and follow the **Din** [the law] of the Torah. But if he knows him to be one who, if he is apprised of this, will **rule for himself** and arrest him or return the merchandise to him or not pay him what he owes him, without the assessment of Beth-**Din** [Court], one must take heed in revealing it to him, for in order to rescue himself from forbidden speech, three more conditions must be satisfied -

> **A.** The subject of cheating - That is, how he cheated him, must be known to the tellers themselves, as opposed to their hearing from others that there is cheating in this place, in which instance they are forbidden to tell him.
> **B.** The tellers must be two.
> **C.** The harm caused the cheater by their words must not be greater than that of the **Din** [the law] resulting from their words in **Beth-Din** [Court]. But if they know the nature of the cheated one to be such that he would cause the cheater a greater loss than that determined by the **Din** [the law] and that he would not abide afterward by the **Din** [the law] for the cheater, it is forbidden to reveal it to him in any case.

And with the first five conditions, there are, altogether, eight conditions -for revealing it. And even if they all coincide, this avails only to rescue oneself from forbidden speech. But, in any event, he does not rescue himself from the **Issur** [prohibition] of **abetting transgression**. For, according to the **Din** [the law], it is forbidden for the hearer to do anything according to their words, even if many speakers told him, so long as they did not testify against him in **Beth-Din** [Court] and **Beth-Din** [Court] have permitted him to do so is above[58]. Therefore, one must be extremely careful not to reveal anything to a person whose nature is to **rule for himself** without the permission of **Beth-Din** [Court]. And now, my brother, see, how in our many sins, so many people stumble so in this, that when one takes merchandise from a store and acquires it with **Meshichah** [a mode of acquisition], according to the **Din** [the law], and shows it to his friend, asking him if it is worth what he paid for it, not only does he not praise it, but he even demeans it, saying - **He really cheated you**. And he is not careful at the time to determine its current market price. Very often the price changes in a short time. And he is also - not careful to determine, how much he overcharged him, whether or not it is an admissible overcharge according to the **Din** [the law] of the Torah. And also, when he overcharged him. Perhaps the time for showing it to a merchant or to a relative has already passed, so that any protest would be of no avail. But he would only be injecting great hatred into the ear of the buyer against the seller, and thereby be a literal **talebearer**, **peddling** talk from one to the other. And many times, he speaks against him out of hatred, and it becomes clear afterward that it is worth what he paid for it. And quite often the seller caused a great loss, for

---

[58] Principle 6, sections 9 and 10

he will incite - the buyer, saying - Go return the Merchandise and throw it in his face. And if you are ashamed to do it yourself, send it to someone else. And if he does not want to take it back, don't pay him what you owe him for this merchandise or - what you owe him from before. And very often this is against the **Din** [the law] and is actual theft and extortion. And when he returns the merchandise to the seller and he refuses to take it, saying that he is causing him a loss according to the **Din** [the law] of the Torah, they come to quarrel and greatly abuse each other. See how many evils this talebearer has committed - He has transgressed the negative commandment of - You shall not go **Rachil** [talebearing] among your people. if he does not pay heed to the aforementioned conditions, and he has transgressed - You shall not place a stumbling block before the blind, in counseling his friend to return the merchandise unlawfully or in causing - other losses and in generating quarrels leading to the transgression of - You shall not wrong, one man, his fellow, and to transgressions of many other negative commandments that result from quarreling, Heaven preserve us. And if so, how much must one take care not to intervene in such things without reflecting well upon what we have written above? And then the Lord will be with him so that nothing adverse will result from his counsel.

Seif 14

If something wrong was done to **Reuven** without his knowing, who did it, **Reuven** came and asked **Shimon** - Who did this to me? even though he understands that **Reuven** suspects him of this, he is forbidden to tell him the name of the doer, even if he saw it - the deed himself. But he should answer - I did not do the thing unless it were a thing which even if he did not suspect him of at all, and which, even if he did not ask him, he would have to tell him himself, as when all of the conditions mentioned at the beginning of this section were met and as we wrote above[59], and as was explained above[60] in respect to **Lashon Hara** [slander]. All of the considerations mentioned there in the book **Mekor Hachaim** and in the book **Be'er Mayim Chayim**, both with respect to the **Din** [the law] and to satisfy the demands of Heaven apply here too.

Seif 15
And now we shall come to explain what many people stumble in. I will give one illustration, from which the intelligent reader will be able to deduce the parallels. It is common for one to bring merchandise to the city to sell, and many buyers come to him. And it often happens that one who has no money with him at the time chooses merchandise and asks the seller not to sell it to another, for he is going to bring him the money. In the interim, other merchants come to him and implore him to sell them the merchandise that the first has selected, and he agrees. Afterward, when the first returns and asks for the merchandise that he selected in the beginning, he answers - **Ploni** [so and so] came, and I did not want to give it to him, but he threw down the money and took it, and against my will, I took it, because I did not want to argue with him. In this case, the seller transgresses the absolute

---

[59] Section 7
[60] Part One, Principle 10, section 17

negative commandment of - You shall not go **Rachil** [talebearing] among your people. Even though a great wrong was committed by the one who implored him to give him the merchandise that the first had selected, still, since he sold it to him and received the money from him, it is certainly a valid sale and no good will come of his revealing the implorer's name; but he will only be injecting hatred into his - the first one's, heart against him - the second, and this is absolute **Rechiluth** [Gossip] as stated above[61]. And this **Din** [the law] is similar in all its details to that of the aforementioned section 14. How much more so - is this the **Din** [the law] in view of what we find very often, that the second did not implore him that much, and that the seller did not inform him that he had already committed himself to the other and that it was only for his own good that he had sold him this merchandise, whatever his reason may have been. And so that the first buyer does not have any complaint against him that he breaks his word, he removes the wrong from himself and imputes it to the other. Certainly, this is a very grave sin, in the category of **Motzi Shem Ra** [one who spreads an evil report], and there apply to it all the negative and positive commandments that we explained in the introduction. And he must take great heed in such an instance not to reveal the name of the second buyer who bought the merchandise, even if this seller wishes to take the wrong upon himself and say - It was my mistake, he knew nothing about your having concluded with me first. For it is very common that even - if explained, in such a way, he injects hatred in his - the first buyer's heart against the second buyer, thinking about him that he

---

[61] Principle 1, section 3

threatened his livelihood. Rather, the seller should answer him plainly - I sold it to another by mistake. And know that all we have written in this book about the great care that must be taken against the transgression of **Lashon Hara** [slander] applies only to one who is still in the category of **your fellow**. But as to those people who deny the Torah of the Lord, even only one letter -of it, and those who mock the words of **Chazal** [Sages], it is a Mitzvah to publicize their deceitful views before all, and to demean them, so that others not learn from their evil deeds.

CHOFETZ Part Two CHAIM

Illustrations

Illustration 1

If **Ploni** [so and so] sees that **Reuven** wants to enter into partnership with **Shimon**, and Shimon does not know Reuven's nature, and **Ploni** [so and so] knows **Reuven** well from the past - that he is indifferent to the money of others because of his bad nature - he should warn Shimon from the beginning not to enter into partnership with him, and there is no **Lashon Hara** [slander] in this. But in this, too, he must take great care that none of the conditions mentioned above[1] are lacking.

---

[1] Principle 9, section 2

Illustration 2

But if **Reuven** already entered into a partnership with Shimon because he did not know him, and **Ploni** [so and so] knew **Reuven's** nature, as mentioned before, it [the din] depends upon this: If **Ploni** [so and so] knows that his words will not be accepted by **Shimon**, except to suspect **Reuven** alone - that is, not to rely exclusively upon **Reuven** from now on in business dealings and inaccurate accounting, but to check everything along with him so that he not come to lose. **Ploni** [so and so] must reveal it to **Shimon**. But in this, too, he must take great care that the conditions mentioned in section 2 not be lacking. But if he sees that his words will be implicitly believed by **Shimon** and will thereby lead to actual loss to **Reuven** - that is, that **Shimon** will annul his partnership with him or other kinds of loss, it is forbidden to reveal it to **Shimon**.

Illustration 3

And know further that he must be very careful not to counsel Reuven to enter into partnership with Shimon if he knows of any loss that might result from their partnership - as when Shimon is very poor, how much more so if he is not trustworthy. The same applies to seeking a **Shidduch** [match] or a craftsman or the like. For even in the instances in which it is forbidden to go and speak **Rechiluth** [Gossip] against Shimon, such as going and saying against him before Reuven, that he is in straitened circumstances, as mentioned above - and, likewise, in respect to a **Shidduch** [match] or a craftsman, each in its own way, it is forbidden to do so only by harming Shimon -

But the opposite; that is, to harm **Reuven** and to counsel him to enter into a partnership or into a **Shidduch** [match] with Shimon, and the like - if he **Ploni** [so and so] knew in himself that if he were in the same position - as Reuven, as when he required the same things, he would distance himself from such people in Shimon's circumstances - it is an absolute **Issur** [prohibition] to counsel **Reuven** in this direction, it being in the category of - You shall not place a stumbling block before the blind, of which **Chazal** [Sages] have said - Do not give him counsel which is inappropriate for him. And there are people who stumble in this because of their self-interest. This is a grave sin, money-lust causing them to transgress a negative commandment of the Torah.

Illustration 4

If **Ploni** [so and so] sees that one wants to make a match with another and he **Ploni** [so and so] knows that the groom has great failings the nature of which will be explained below[2], and the father of the prospective bride knows nothing about it, and if he did know, he would not consent, he should be told. But he who looks into it should know that there are in this din many details, which we shall explain below, and he must take all of them into consideration before he permits this to himself. He should also not deduce leniencies for himself from one situation to another. And before we begin to explain this din in all its details, we shall attempt to remove the common stumbling locks in this area though, to speak the truth, there is no need to mention them in a book, for they are very obvious and require neither learning nor reasoning. But because of the great harm wrought by them and because they are regarded as permitted by many individuals, I have been constrained to explain the great deception of **the men of the tongue** in this regard. Perhaps the Lord will grant the removal of some of this great blindness. And this I begin with the help of the Lord.

---

[2] section 6

Illustration 5

Great care must be taken to avoid those base traits which cause one party to the **Shidduch** [match] to be demeaned before the second party for completely insubstantial things. So that - for example if the - prospective groom were an innocent person, who was not so sharp as to understand the subtleties of men and their deceits, or who did not want to engage in levity like the other youths of his age, he is immediately publicized in the city as a fool and a simpleton, so that sometimes this will be a reason for others not to want to make a match with him, or to break the match that they have already made, and many other such wrongs - May the Lord cut off such **slippery lips** for this For it does not suffice them that they are in the category of - men of **Lashon Hara** [slander] because of this - for in these words of vanity and their like there is not found even one particular of those mentioned above[3] - but the Torah even calls them **spreaders of false reports** because what they say is false, as we have written above[4] on this subject. And even if what they said were the absolute truth, it would require all of the aforementioned conditions.

And in truth, these people are also in the category of **Machtiei Harabim** [people causing the many to sin]. For because of this evil nature of theirs, whereby they hasten to mock people and to pour out shame and disgrace upon them they compel men who are pure and just in their hearts to follow in their paths - in the beginning, by force, so that those scoffers and **men of the tongue** not

---

[3] Principle 9, section 2
[4] Part One, Principle 1, and in Principle 5

publicize them as fools and simpletons or brand them as **hypocrites**, and then, as a matter of course, they are dragged after them, for **habit becomes nature**. And, as per the well-known dictum in the Talmud[5] on the verse - Happy[6] is the man who has not followed the counsel of the wicked or taken the path of sinners, or joined the company of the insolent. with the scoffers, he is destined to stand with them, and if he stands with them, he is destined to sit with them....

And how much must one strengthen himself not to give these people an opening in the beginning; that is, not to argue with them, but to strengthen himself greatly not to associate himself with them at all, as it is written - If[7] they say Come with us Let us set an ambush to shed blood Let us lie in wait for the innocent. Like[8] Sheol let us swallow them alive whole like those who go down into the Pit. We[9] shall obtain every precious treasure we shall fill our homes with loot. Throw[10] in your lot with us we shall all have a common purse. My[11] son do not set out with them keep your feet from their path. For[12] their feet run to evil they hurry to shed blood. And **Chazal** [Sages] have said in the Mishna - Better[13] that a man be called a fool all of his days and not be wicked one moment before the Lord. **Called a fool** is stated because of the matter discussed there; but in truth, it befits a man to commit

---

[5] Avodah Zarah 18b
[6] Psalms 1:1
[7] Mishlei 1:11
[8] Mishlei 1:12
[9] Mishlei 1:13
[10] Mishlei 1:14
[11] Mishlei 1:15
[12] Mishlei 1:16
[13] Eduyoth 5:6

folly, even actively, so that the epithet **wicked** not apply to him, even for one moment, above. As we find in Scripture on the verse[14] - that David made himself act like a fool in the house of **Avimelech** so that he not falls into his hands. How much more so - should one follow this stratagem, if necessary, for the sake of the King of kings, the Holy One Blessed be He. And in the Talmud[15] about the verse - Man[16] and beast do You save, O Lord - these are men who are wise in knowledge, but who make themselves act foolish like a beast for the sake of the Lord. And see the Talmud -If[17] one finds **S'haatnez** [A garment made of wool and linen] in his garment, etc.

And, likewise, to shame one of the parties to a **Shidduch** [match] because of the deeds of his forbears - this, too, is in the category of **Lashon Hara** [slander], as explained above[18].

---

[14] Samuel-A 21:16
[15] Chullin 5b
[16] Psalms 36:7
[17] Berachoth 19b
[18] Principle 4

CHOFETZ   Illustrations   CHAIM

Illustration 6

And now we shall return to explain what we permitted at the beginning of section 4, in an instance of the prospective groom's having great defects. For there is a difference between the defects. That is, if the defect is with respect to a bodily ill that the father of the prospective bride is unaware of, it being something internal that is not revealed to all, it is obvious that the one who reveals this is not suspect of any **Issur** [prohibition] of **Rechiluth** [Gossip] so long as none of the conditions mentioned above[19]. And I have explained them here in the book **Be'er Mayim Chayim**.

And there is yet another instance in which he must reveal it to him. If it is heard about the groom that there is **Apikorsuth** [heresy] in him, God forbid, it must be revealed to him. And about this it is stated in juxtaposition - You[20] shall not go talebearing among your people. but - Do[21] not stand by the blood of your friend.

But if the defect is with respect to the little Torah wisdom that he possesses, this is not to be revealed to him. For he the prospective father-in-law **caused his own loss**. For he should have taken him to men of Torah to test him in the strength of his wisdom and his knowledge, and if he did this, they the testers must tell the truth, for both parties had agreed upon this in the beginning, and, not having done so it is understood that he has acquiesced in the matter.

Aside from all this, one who would want to permit

---

[19] Principle 9, section 2
[20] Vayikra 19:16
[21] Vayikra 19:16

this revelation because he cannot look on at his friend being cheated by the **Shadchanim** [the matchmakers] deceiving the prospective father-in-law, must assure himself first that the amount of the dowry and the food and clothing allotment agreed to by the father-in-law is a true commitment and he will not deceive. For, in general, one should not hasten to permit this. For our eyes see that many of them do not honor their commitments, and if so, the phenomenon of **cheating** does not apply here. For just as the groom to deceive the father-in-law-to-be, so does the father-in-law deceive him, and they end off as **equals**. And, aside from all this, here, too, all of the conditions mentioned above[22] must be satisfied.

---

[22] Principle 9, section 2

Illustration 7

The same holds true for revealing to the groom the affairs of the father-in-law. That is, if he knows of an internal illness of the betrothed but they are concealing it from the groom, the revealer is not suspect of the **Issur** [prohibition] of **Rechiluth** [Gossip] but the required conditions must be met.

Similarly, if it was heard about the house of his prospective father-in-law that it is a house of **Pritzuth** [immodesty] - and it is well known that this is a great cause for missing the desired end of the marriage - in this instance, too, the thing must be revealed, and in this, the aforementioned conditions for revelation] do not obtain. But he the potential revealer must first reflect upon whether his words will be heeded, for in a **Shidduch** [match] it is very often found that they are not heeded, and it is inevitable that in such an instance revelation will lead only to **Rechiluth** [Gossip].

Illustration 8

But if he knows that the father-in-law is deceiving the groom in the matter of the dowry and the food allotment, he must take great counsel with himself before he reveals it to the groom. This requires several considerations -

>**A.** He must reflect well to determine if he is really cheating him. That is, he must be convinced of his bad nature or the soreness of his poverty, or to have heard from him explicitly that he commits himself only outwardly. And he should not conclude immediately to think about the father-in-law that because he is in straitened circumstances, he certainly will not give him the dowry or the food allotment that he promised. For do we not see many times that men like these pay their debts more readily than the exalted householders?
>
>**B.** To reveal it, he must know that if the groom knew about it, he would not consent to the **Shidduch** [match]. Very often it happens that the groom only wants to get from the father-in-law as much as he can, but the **Shidduch** [match] itself is not affected by this at all. And in such an instance, there is certainly no **Heter** [a halachic permit] to go and reveal it to him unless he sees that his words will be of benefit to the groom, that he will take counsel on how to get securities from the father-in-law for this.
>
>**C.** To reveal it, he must know that on the part of the groom, there will be no deception. For if the groom, too, is deceiving him in aught, they emerge as **equals**, and it is obvious that it is forbidden to

reveal it.

Aside from this, all the aforementioned conditions must be met. Therefore, he should not hasten to reveal it unless after intensive reflection whether all of the necessary requirements have been satisfied.

Illustration 9

And if the groom has already made the **Shidduch** [match] and he the potential revealer knows that the father-in-law will deceive the groom in the matter of the dowry or the food allotment, the **Din** [the law] depends on this - If he sees that his words will be accepted by the groom only to the extent of suspicion alone. That is, he will seek counsel against the father-in-law so as not to be deceived by him. Or if he knows that the groom will do nothing by himself but only with **Beth-Din** [Court], it is permitted to reveal it to him. But he must take care that none of the conditions explained above[23] are lacking. It would also seem that he must also satisfy clause c above. That is, he must know that on the groom's part, there is no deception. But if he sees that his words will be accepted by the groom and that because of this he will peremptorily annul the **Shidduch** [match] by himself, it is forbidden to reveal it to him; for it is not common for all the needed conditions to coincide. See in the book **Be'er Mayim Chayim**.

---

[23] Principle 9, section 2

Illustration 10

And sometimes it is conceivable that it is permitted to reveal it, as when he knows that the bride has an internal illness which is not known to all, including the groom. But he must take care that all the conditions mentioned above[24] are satisfied.

And if he the potential revealer did not know the thing by himself but only heard it from others, he should not reveal it, unless he feels that the groom will not do anything by himself to dissolve the **Shidduch** [match], but will only suspect and investigate carefully. And in this, too, the conditions explained above[25] must be satisfied.

---

[24] Principle 9, section 2
[25] Principle 9, section 2

Illustration 11

And if he knows that the father-in-law's house is a house of **Pritzuth** [immodesty], he must reveal it. And if he knows that there is **Apikorsuth** [heresy] in the groom, it is certainly a Mitzvah to reveal it, and none of the aforementioned conditions need be satisfied. And even if he does not know this by himself, but heard it from others, he must still reveal it. But he must take care not to reveal it in such a way that gives the impression that he knows the thing by himself, but he must state plainly - I have heard this and this. Even though this is not to be believed implicitly as yet, it should be suspected and investigated.

I had intended to furnish additional illustrations concerning craftsmen, hired men, servants, and the like. But because of high printing expenses and time contingencies, I was prevented from doing so. In sum - A man must set his eyes and his heart on his ways, and especially on the utterances of his mouth, not to become involved in affairs **between man and his neighbor** unless he knows thoroughly the matter to be dealt with, to intend benefit only, not to be motivated by hatred, and to foresee the fruits of his speech, that it not breaks the bounds of din, God forbid. And then the Lord will be his hope that he will not be ensnared in the net of the evil inclination. And the Rock of Israel will rescue him from error, and He will show him wonders from His Torah.

www.ingramcontent.com/pod-product-compliance
Lightning Source LLC
Chambersburg PA
CBHW070138080526
44586CB00015B/1744